# The
# Gift
## of
# Stories

# The
# Gift
## of
# Stories

Practical and Spiritual
Applications of Autobiography,
Life Stories, and
Personal Mythmaking

Robert Atkinson

**Bergin & Garvey**
Westport, Connecticut • London

**Library of Congress Cataloging-in-Publication Data**

Atkinson, Robert
    The gift of stories : practical and spiritual applications of
autobiography, life stories, and personal mythmaking / Robert
Atkinson.
       p.    cm.
    Includes bibliographical references and index.
    ISBN 0–89789–430–8 (hc : alk. paper).—ISBN 0–89789–443–X (pbk :
alk. paper)
    1. Mythology—Psychology. 2. Personal narratives.
3. Storytelling—Psychological aspects. 4. Self-discovery.
I. Title.
BL313.A86    1995
158–dc20     94–39208

British Library Cataloguing in Publication Data is available.

Library of Congress Catalog Card Number: 94–39208

ISBN: 0–89789–430–8
    0–89789–443–X (pbk.)

First published in 1995

Bergin & Garvey, 88 Post Road West, Westport, CT 06881
An imprint of Greenwood Publishing Group, Inc.

Printed in the United States of America

♾™

The paper used in this book complies with the
Permanent Paper Standard issued by the National
Information Standards Organization (Z39.48–1984).

10  9  8  7  6  5

**Copyright Acknowledgment**

The author and publisher gratefully acknowledge permission to reprint the following copy-
righted material:

Extract from Arlo Guthrie, "My Oughtabiography," *Rolling Blunder Review*, November 1989.
Copyright © 1989 by Arlo Guthrie. Used with permission of the Guthrie Center.

# Contents

# *Exhibits*

# *Acknowledgments*

Just as every story has more than one character, every book has more than one author, even if it doesn't say so on the cover. My appreciation goes to all those who have played important and distinct roles in making this book what it is. Specifically, I want to thank my guides, mentors, and friends who have introduced me to the wonder of stories, allowed me to live some remarkable stories with them, and supported my interests in various ways: Bruce Buckley, Pete Seeger, Jack Elliott, Arlo Guthrie, Joseph Campbell, Father Jeremiah, Peter Fernald, Angelo Boy, Dwight Webb, Richard Katz, Henry Glassie, Brian Sutton-Smith, Ken Goldstein, Bert Cohler, Will Callander, Dorothy Moore, Mike Brady, Robert Coles, Kit Ward, and Pam Smith.

I also want to thank the Spencer Foundation for a small grant to interview teenagers for their life stories, an important early project of the Center for the Study of Lives at the University of Southern Maine, and the USM Faculty Senate Research Fund for their support.

I especially want to thank the hundreds of students in my classes who have played such a key role in the creation of this book by sharing of themselves and telling their truth so clearly. I particularly thank those whose stories appear in this book: Shirley Barlow, Merrill Bittner, Kathy Bonney, Esther Cole, Victoria Correale, Dyan Dyer, Victoria Heflin, Rebecca Hotaling, Thalia Drake Jillson, Diane Johnson, Diana Jordan, Diane Nicole Piaget, and Joan Tankey.

# *Introduction*

Long ago, people spent the best times of their lives telling each other stories. It was a magic time, a time when the animals spoke a language that people could understand, and children were sometimes born with wings. It was a time when the land, the sea, and the sky sang love songs back and forth, and a time when men and women lived in harmony with each other.

Mothers and fathers would rock their children in their arms, spinning tales of where they came from before birth and where they would go when their bodies wore out. Everybody gathered around fires at night to listen to the elders tell how everything came into being, how the seasons followed one another, and how the dawn chased away darkness.

It was through these stories that girls learned what it meant to be women and boys learned what it meant to be men. Stories were the center of community life. They gave everything a reason for being and told of the sacredness of all life.

But one cold, harsh winter, an evil wind blew across the land, snuffing out the evening fires and taking everything else with it, including the delicate web of stories that bound mothers to daughters, fathers to sons, neighbors to neighbors. No one was able to remember the old stories any more. The people felt aimless. Worst of all, everyone had forgotten that they were all storymakers.

Then, in the spring, someone wrote down their own story. And someone else wrote down their story. Pretty soon their stories were printed, and other people read them. Then radio came along, and soon after that television, and people began listening to and watching other people's stories.

But then one day, someone told their own story to someone else and it felt good. Another person told their story to someone else, and that felt good, too. More and more people started telling their stories to each other. Soon all the people were feeling much better again. And the strangest thing happened; they began to remember some of the old stories. They discovered that their own stories mirrored the stories originally told about the gods and goddesses, and they found their direction again. They felt linked together again. Once in awhile, there was even a child born with wings. Best of all, everyone remembered that they all were storymakers, all with lots of precious tales to share. And everyone remembered, too, that stories lead from and back to the sacredness of life.[1]

That's a storyteller's history of the world, as well as, the story of why this book was written. Storytelling is in our blood. It is part of our nature. Today, we are living in a spiritual springtime. Ours is a time, as Carl Jung has said, of a "metamorphosis of the gods."[2] We are recognizing more readily now that there is something of the gods and goddesses inside us, too. Ours is a time of healing, of purging, of acceptance, of honoring, and of renewal. Telling our stories is helping this to come about. This book is designed to assist you in becoming the storymaker you were born to become.

People everywhere are telling stories about some piece of their lives to friends and strangers alike. Putting our life's events into the form of a story, even as a written narrative, can help us bear a burden or see with a clearer perspective. The stories of our lives carry a great power because we tap into ageless, universal themes that become deeply familiar to us when we tell our stories. Our stories are always variations of one of the thousands of folk tales, myths, or legends, that have spoken to us for generations of our inner truths. Stories connect us to our roots.

This inner need to tell our stories has spawned the new discipline of journal therapy, where you tell your innermost and even darkest thoughts to your journal without fear of judgment. As a silent listener, our journal accepts everything.[3] Twelve-step recovery programs, such as Alcoholics Anonymous, Adult Children of Alcoholics, and Co-Dependents Anonymous, have known all along that telling a personal narrative can be very therapeutic. They understand the transforming power of telling our stories, and being listened to nonjudgmentally. They make survival and recovery stories, which are the heart and soul of myth, a central part of the recovery process. Those in a program tell and listen to each other's stories describing what happened and how the change occurred. This kind of storytelling validates each person's experience and restores value to people's lives who might have known only suppression. It can also allow old, forgotten dreams to be reclaimed.

Telling our stories strengthens family and community bonds. With so many families living so far apart today, and so many others still suffering from the effects of various hurts over the years spent together, any chance to reminisce and tell family stories is a wonderful opportunity. Any story about a family member that is told and retold becomes a family story carrying important messages and informal rules. These stories give a family definition and provide it with esteem and often an ideal to live up to. Families and other groups who tell children the stories of parents' and grandparents' lives have become "communities of memory."[4] Sharing personally significant stories in groups like this sustains hope for the future.

Stories have also gained respect and acceptance in academia. Psychologists now see the value of personal narratives in understanding growth and development. Anthropologists use the life history, or the individual case study, as the preferred unit of study for their measures of cultural similarities and variations. Literary scholars and teachers of English use autobiography in the classroom and in their own research as texts through which to explore questions of design, style, content, literary themes, and personal truth. Historians find in using the oral history approach that life story materials are an important source for enhancing local history.

Life storytelling also teaches us about our spiritual self, about our personal quest for wholeness and authenticity. We have become intrigued by everything "spiritual." We want to know who we are at our core; we want to connect with our spirit and with others. Everything we encounter as adults that gives us a new and deeper meaning in life is spiritual. Most of our growth during adulthood is psychospiritual. This includes our experiences of real intimacy and creativity, how we deal with life crises like death and divorce, as well as our peak experiences. In seeking our spiritual selves, we seek to understand what matters most to us, what is personally sacred. Telling the stories of our life is telling our spiritual autobiography, because this helps us discover, and become more aware of, what our deepest values are and what we can put our fullest trust in. We come to realize that even struggles and conflicts have their place because they have served an important purpose over time.

We become fully aware, fully conscious of our lives through story. Reclaiming story is part of our birthright. Telling our own story enables us to speak our truth and to be heard, recognized, and acknowledged by others. It is *only* through story that our truth can be told, that the meaning of life can be identified. Story makes the implicit explicit, the hidden seen, the unformed formed, and the confusing clear. Jerome Bruner, a leading cognitive psychologist turned narrative psychologist, in speaking about the new interest in the study of life writing, said recently, "Few questions have a longer, deeper, and livelier intellectual history than how we *construct* our lives—and, indeed, how we create ourselves in the process."[5]

*The Gift of Stories* was written to help you construct and create the story of your life, step by step, from the unique to the universal level of self-expression. It shows why and how stories interpret life, and how you can learn to trust, reclaim, and share your experience while moving from storymaking to mythmaking to soulmaking.

The purpose of this book is to provide you with some practical reasons and guidelines for finding, organizing, making coherent, sharing, and appreciating the story of your life, while helping you understand your life within the universal framework of mythology. It also takes this process a step further by providing guidelines for you to assist someone else in telling their life story.

The book is organized around the theme that storytelling can transform our lives. It is designed to help facilitate a natural developmental process of personal transformation. The first part of the book explains why storytelling transforms our lives. Chapter 1 makes it clear why knowing our stories is essential, what the emotional impact of telling the stories of our lives can be like, and examines the power of stories by illustrating the four transforming functions built into the stories we tell. Chapter 2 shows why sacred stories held traditional communities together, and how they got their transforming power from the timeless elements they contain. Chapter 3 helps us become familiar with the sacred elements of stories by taking a close look at the blueprint or pattern all well-told stories follow, which prepares us to see the sacred in our own stories.

The second part of the book shows how we can use storytelling as a process for bringing about transformation in ourselves and others. Each step of this process utilizes different skills that move us to a deeper level of emotional and spiritual involvement. Chapter 4 provides guided exercises for writing autobiographically, to help us recognize the themes and patterns of our lives and give us a deeper awareness of ourselves. Chapter 5 offers guided exercises for personal mythmaking, to help us connect our lives to ageless mythic themes and those who have gone before us, while giving our life deeper meaning by enabling us to tell our own life experience as a sacred story. Chapter 6, on merging our personal myth with the guiding myth of our time, helps us find the knowledge of our part in the larger whole and the volition to bring our deeper purpose into being. Chapter 7 enables us to give the gift of storytelling, by guiding others in telling their life stories. In so doing, we take action upon our new knowledge of ourselves in the world and practice what we have learned while being of service to others.

The book focuses on the three forms of personal stories: life story, autobiography, and personal myth. A *life story*[6] is the story a person chooses to tell about the life they have lived, what they remember of it, and what they want others to know of it. A life story is the essence of what has happened to us. It can cover the time from birth or before to the present and beyond. It includes the important events, experiences, and feelings of a lifetime. It can be written or told orally to another (an interviewer). I would include memoir, journaling, autobiography, and doing a life story interview with another person as forms of life stories.

There is very little difference between a life story, a life history, and oral history. The first two are usually different terms for the same thing. An oral history, however, more often focuses on a specific aspect of the person's life, such as work life or special role in some part of the life of a community, where the focus is most often the community or what someone remembers about a specific event, issue, time, or place.

A life story can take a poetic form, a factual form, a metaphorical form, or any other creatively expressive form. What is important is that the life story be told in the form, shape, and style that is most comfortable to the person telling it. Whatever form it takes, a life story always brings order and meaning to the life being told, for both the teller and the listener. It is a way to greater self-understanding, a way to leave a personal legacy for the future. A life story is a fairly complete rendering of one's entire experience of life as a whole, highlighting the most important aspects.

An *autobiography*[7] is a more formal, written story of a person's life. No longer are autobiographies written only by older people. We live in an age when anybody at anytime feels comfortable writing an autobiography. This term is sometimes used interchangeably with life story. Autobiographical writing can also consist of shorter exercises or written pieces that focus on one event or memory in a person's life, such as a key childhood experience or an important transition (see chapter 4). These short pieces may or may not be put together to form one's complete autobiography.

A *personal myth*[8] is what is most deeply true about our own experience of life. It is our expression of those personally sacred and timeless elements of our lives. It focuses on the experiences, beliefs, motifs, and themes of a lifetime that have ordered, shaped, and directed our lives. Personal myth-making is the process of recognizing, understanding, and embracing the ways archetypal, or universal, themes and motifs play themselves out in our life experiences. A personal myth is made up of the same three parts that form a traditional story or classical myth. It is our personal expression of how the pattern of separation-initiation-return has played itself out in our life. (Chapters 3 and 5 provide in-depth explanation of this process.) This is what links the individual story we have lived to the collective story we all share. The personal myth teaches us about the universality of life.

Sharing all forms of life stories is a powerful experience, one that can touch us deeply and give us great joy and satisfaction. It can give us a sense of inner harmony and connectedness. The real idea of a life story is to enable idividuals to express their truth, as they see it, so that others might learn from it. What people typically choose to include in their life story are the constructive, or healing, aspects of their life and experience rather than allowing destructive elements to become the focus, as is often the case in biography. The movement toward life stories, where we tell our own story in our own words, is a movement toward perpetuating healing stories.

To paraphrase Brother Blue, the African-American storyteller, "Enough stories can change the world." That is, enough truthful stories—from the heart, of the soul—can stop hatred, prejudice, racism, and this *can* change the world. By hearing one's own and another's truths, we become more in tune with, more sensitive to, and more connected to each other. The more life stories that are shared between people everywhere and from all backgrounds, the closer we will all become. As Maya Angelou has written, in her poem *Human Family*, "We are more alike, my friends, than we are unalike."[9]

One more thing before you embark upon this journey of self-exploration: you may want to prepare your own space where you can do the work of thinking about, creating, and writing your story. Have your writing materials (or your computer, if you write on a computer) ready as you go through each of the chapters in this book so you will be able to put down your thoughts as you go along.

## NOTES

1. This story was inspired by a story in the article, "Once upon a time . . . " by Anne Chapman.
2. Jung, *The undiscovered self,* pp. 119, 123.
3. Solly and Lloyd, *Journey notes,* pp. 1–17.
4. Robert Bellah, et al., *Habits of the heart,* pp. 152–155.
5. Quoted in Josselson and Lieblich, *The narrative study of lives,* back cover.
6. See Ives, Symposium on the life story; and Jeff Titon, The life story.
7. See Olney (ed.), *Autobiography;* and Birren and Hedlund, Contributions of autobiography.
8. See Jung, *Memories, dreams, reflections,* p. 3; Feinstein and Krippner, *Personal mythology;* and Stephen Larsen, *The mythic imagination.*
9. Angelou, *I shall not be moved.*

# I

# THE POWER OF STORIES

My friend, I am going to tell you the story of my life, as you wish; and if it were only the story of my life I think I would not tell it; for what is one man that he should make much of his winters, even when they bend him like a heavy snow?

It is the story of all life that is holy and is good to tell, and of us two-leggeds sharing in it with the four-leggeds and the wings of the air and all green things; for these are children of one mother and their father is one spirit.

Black Elk, from John Neihardt, *Black Elk Speaks*

# 1

## *Understanding the Transforming Functions of Stories*

A story can possess an immediacy, as it connects so persuasively with human experience.[1]

Stories—those that have been told across the generations, as well as our own—inform, inspire, teach, maintain moral codes, record events that become history, establish family lines and geneology, preserve customs, guide us, show us possibilities, open our hearts, make us laugh, and clarify all aspects of life while healing and transforming. We are, all of us, living stories, eager to find our own voices by which we can be known to others.

Story is a tool for making us whole; stories gather up the parts of us and put them together in a way that gives our lives greater meaning than they had before we told our story. Story is a tool for self-discovery; stories tell us new things about ourselves that we wouldn't have been as aware of without having told the story.

There is a power in storytelling that can transform our lives. Traditional stories, myths, and fairy tales hold this power. Stories told from generation to generation carry this power in the enduring values and lessons about living life deeply that they pass on. This is what makes myth and scriptural stories so powerful and sacred. A sacred story draws us right into the timelessness of human experience by connecting us with what is most essentially human, at the same time enabling us to see our own experience more clearly.

The transforming power of traditional stories lies in their sacred, enduring elements that show us how our experience is linked to that of other human beings. Myth, folk tales, and other sacred stories fulfill their purpose when they illustrate that our own experience or situation in life is not unique but rather common to others—and timeless, as well.

The stories we tell of our own lives carry this transforming power, too. The stories within us contain the same timeless elements. Our stories illustrate our inherent connectedness with others. The stories of our lives are sacred even before we realize it, because they are all guided by the same underlying cultural patterns and enduring elements that tie us all together as human beings. When we become aware of these lasting, universally human elements in our own stories, we recognize their sacredness. The more familiar we are with these enduring elements of traditional stories, the better we become at recognizing these same elements in our own life stories.

In the life story of each person is a reflection of another's life story. In some mysterious, amazing way our stories and our lives are all tied together. A life story gives us the benefit of seeing how one person experiences and understands life over time. In telling our life story, we gain new insights into human dilemmas, human struggles, and human triumphs, while also gaining a greater appreciation for how values and beliefs are acquired, shaped, and held onto. In this way, the story of one person can become the story of us all.

We discover in the process of telling our life stories that we are more sacred beings than we are human beings. A life story is really the story of the soul of a person. The most powerful life story expresses the struggle of a soul living in a material world. The most important stories we tell about ourselves are those that express the timeless within us.

The transformation experienced through the telling of our own stories is a gift we can give ourselves at any point in our lives. We can learn to see our lives as a story wherever we are in our lives as long as we are willing to reflect upon our own experience. Telling our story while it is in process, whether we are at the threshold of adulthood or at the midpoint of our lives or later, helps us gain a sharper perspective on our past and our present while also helping us to imagine how the struggle we might be in the middle of could eventually turn out. Telling the stories of our lives can give us a clearer sense of what we really hope for.

There are unforgettable moments in the telling of our stories when we recognize a connection in our lives, a connection that links one moment of our lives with another, maybe years apart, or a moment that connects us in some deep way to our parents, our grandparents, our ancestors, and maybe even to all of humanity. These are moments when our whole perception of ourselves and the world can change instantly. They can occur often when we reflect on and share the stories of our life with others. This is what brings about the immediacy of stories of which Robert Coles speaks. In this moment, new insights take over, and all we want to do is savor the moment and do whatever we can, or have to, not to let anything else interrupt this new connection we have made to ourselves—to our own soul—or to others.

A story told well carries a power that can pull blinders off our eyes. It can teach us something important about life that we had probably forgotten we knew. The act of imposing a narrative framework on the raw material of our lives brings new order and clarity to something somehow familiar to us. A good story allows us to wrestle with our demons, dance with our angels, make plans with our inner guide, and, ultimately, connect with our soul. Telling ourselves and others these deep stories of our lives is doing soul work. It is through stories that symbolic images and universal, timeless themes find their expression. Through this kind of deliberate, soulful expression we come to terms with our own experience, our own life, in relation to others.

Telling our life stories also provides us with an opportunity to exercise our imagination or unleash our fantasies. This can have an important role in constructing the self-image or identity we want for ourselves. When we use our imagination, we use our power to form mental images not of what is actually present but of what we would like to be present. Image and imagination are both from the same root, *imago*, which is a likeness or copy of what we envision. When we tell stories, we sometimes create new mental images of things that never actually were but that help us become who we want to be by integrating previous experiences into a form that makes more sense to us combined than did the individual elements. This is using our inner creative power to make stories with the power to transform ourselves.

One time, a woman explained to me that she had had a difficult time with a storytelling exercise I'd assigned, one on the unique moment of her birth. Her childhood as the daughter of an alcoholic was just too painful for her to think about. I gave her permission to think creatively about her situation, and to use her imagination in coming up with something she could feel good about.

The following week, she showed me her story. She was born during World War II; her father was in the service and did not see his new daughter for about a year. When he came back he became an alcoholic, couldn't trust women, and didn't talk to his daughter. She saw her early years as a "constant war between my father, my mother and me." She often wondered what kind of life she would have had were alcohol not a problem in her family. She ended her narrative with the statement: "My father committed suicide August 3, 1979, my mother died of a brain tumor November 17, 1979. I was born November 18, 1979."

In her writing was her resolution. She used her imagination in a very positive way to create a new—and symbolic—story that expressed a truth about her life. She utilized a resourcefulness in bringing order to some confusing experiences in her life story. Her use of imagination actually brought into her personal story the great and universal theme of rebirth, possible only when she recognized and accepted the equally powerful image and role of tragedy in her story.

Life storytelling is a tool for meaning-making. Telling a story about our lives allows us to organize and make clearer what had previously been at best only thoughts in our minds. New meaning in our lives helps heal old wounds that may have been left unattended for a lifetime. This increases self-understanding and self-acceptance.

## THE FOUR FUNCTIONS OF STORIES

Like myths in traditional communities, our own life stories also serve the four classic functions of bringing us more into accord with ourselves, others, the mystery of life, and the universe around us.[2] Traditionally, the socially prescribed rites of passage facilitated this transformation. Following the sacred pattern of *birth, death, rebirth*, they were designed to bring about the desired insights, sentiments, and commitments that would result in a new level of maturity with which the initiate could take on the responsibilities of the new status.

In societies where traditional rites are no longer maintained, the individual still has ritual-like experiences, but on his or her own. The community as a whole may no longer set aside ritual time or structure, but individual experiences of order, trauma, beauty, and exhilaration do occur. When we *consciously* tell about these experiences, communicating our own insights, sentiments, and commitments from the depth of our being, the story will have the power and force of living myth for us as well as our listeners. This is so because mythological symbols—and autobiographical images that emerge from a life lived deeply and consciously—reverberate beyond the personal and into the collective realm. They touch a center of life that we all have within us. This is what enables our stories to fulfill the same four transforming functions of a living mythology. Stories connect us to the psychological, the social, the spiritual-mystical, and the cosmological realms.

### The Psychological Function of Stories

Telling our life stories, with their deeply human elements, is an act of centering and integrating ourselves through gaining a clearer understanding of our experiences, our feelings about them, and their meaning for us. The whole process of psychological development focuses on a dialectic of conflict and resolution, change and growth. To achieve what we are capable of, we need continually to take in and make sense of what we experience. Telling our stories brings order to our experience, and helps us to view our lives both subjectively and objectively at the same time. As we face and reface conflicts that arise, our experiences and feelings merge into a harmony. The more we reflect upon our experience, the more we understand who we are.

Our stories help clarify our experiences, and give us new insights into understanding our lives. Traditional communities fulfilled this function for its members by guiding them through a socially prescribed rite of passage. Since we can no longer rely on our society to bring clarity to our experience, balance to our lives, or unity to the various parts of ourselves, we must find our own way to do this, so we tell our stories. This is why stories have become a central part of the clinical hour. Stories bring meaning to our experience and harmony to our thoughts and feelings. A woman wrote vividly of how she accomplished this inner unity when looking back on one of her earliest memories.

I was four years old, and Larry was my best friend. When everyone was shouting at each other, when the house seemed full of anger and rage, Larry and I would disappear into the backyard. Our backyard was a magical place. It was as close to being in the woods as you could get, fifteen minutes outside of Los Angeles. Our backyard was full of trees; mostly oaks and black walnut trees, sycamores, and the occasional avocado, pomegranate and bay.

Larry and I would always run first to the swing set tucked in a back corner of the yard, just out of sight of the house. We did a lot of talking and dreaming in that back corner of the yard. I was very shy and rarely talked to anyone, except Larry. As we sat in our swings, we were shaded by the fragrant leaves of the old bay tree. We'd grab a leaf and crunch it in our hands, smelling the pungent, magical smell. It was a ritual that set the stage for dreaming.

"What shall we dream today, Larry?"

"Oh," he would say, "let's pretend I'm an orphan with no family and very poor. And I go about the world saving people and helping them be happy, and everyone loves me for it."

"That's a good one, Larry. Who shall we save this time?" And so another tale of strength and perseverance through adversity would begin to wind its way amongst the trees of the bay and walnut and oak.

To the left of the swing set, just over the picket fence with the wrought iron gate which marked the entrance to a deeper part of woods, a solitary redwood tree was making its straight determined way up to the sky. Larry and I used to love to imagine growing up under that tree. We would find a little baby who had been abandoned by her parents and we would take care of her there, under the redwood tree. No one would miss us, and we would live happily in our backyard woods. We would have such a happy, loving family.

Larry and I had a rich and wonderful fantasy world. We hated to leave it. But the call inevitably came: "Itty Bit! Come in now. Where are you? Where have you been? Itty Bit," my mother would continue insistently, "come along now. I want you to meet someone." Or, "I want to take you to the party now and we need to get you clean and pretty."

The real world was such an interruption and a bother. Larry and I would promise our imaginary world that we would return as soon as possible, and then reluctantly we would come out of the woods to face the extroverted world of family and expectations, ever alert to the moment we could slip away again.

"Have you been playing with Larry again?" my sister would mockingly ask. She and my brother loved to make fun of Larry. They were always teasing me about him, and my parents would join in on the laughter. "Larry isn't real, honey," my mother would say, "he's just a pretend friend, an imaginary playmate."

"He is real!" I would shout. "And he is my best friend! He loves me and we want to go away and play!" Then I would cry or run to my room as the others would laugh, or continue to discount this one unconditionally loving and accepting relationship in my life.

As the time for entering kindergarten grew closer, the taunts seemed to grow. It became clear to me that I would constantly be embarrassed and humiliated by my brother and sister about Larry. They would tease me in front of other playmates, who would then join in on the laughter. I couldn't bear the thought of so much mocking attention.

One night, when the rest of the family was out to dinner and the babysitter was downstairs thinking I was all tucked into bed, I realized that Larry was very sick. I decided he was dying and needed medicine. I quietly left my room and went to the bathroom and, stretching up on tiptoes, I found the bottle of baby aspirin. I brought it back to my room and gave all the grainy, orange tasting pills to Larry who was by this time very ill. I put the empty bottle on the floor beside the door to my room, and went back to comfort Larry who now seemed to be slipping away from me.

I awoke to much confusion. It was all bright lights and I was surrounded by strange men who were trying to make me swallow a rubber tube. I wouldn't, so they put it up my nose and pushed it down, down my throat. It was awful. I was screaming, and Larry was gone.

Larry never came back. I never spoke of him again. I entered school, found a playmate or two who were almost as fun at pretending, and best of all, I was no longer teased about having an "imaginary friend."

Forty years later, now living in the woods of Maine, I returned to California to help my stepmother empty out the house for its new owners. Taking a break from sifting through long forgotten treasures and memories, I found my way to the corner of the backyard where the swing set used to be. The old bay tree was still there, its huge, winding branches now supported by metal braces. As I crushed some leaves in my hands, my eyes rested on the redwood tree, now a tower reaching into the sky, and I wept.

I wept for that little girl who felt she had to kill off the strong animus within her, that she had, in her little person's way, been integrating so well into her developing psyche. And I at last wept for Larry, that part of me so long denied, now emerging to complete the whole androgenous person who is me. Welcome home, Larry.

This is a beautiful story of great power, filled with intrigue, drama, adventure, and emotion, told by a very self-aware woman who not only had a rich imagination as a child but also was able to recall that imagination forty years later and reclaim a part of her self that had been forced out of her life before she was ready to let it go. This also illustrates how the principle of gender crossover actually works in real life. For some of us, we are forced to deny our other half, but by midlife we become freer to integrate that part of ourselves and recognize ourselves as the whole beings we were meant to be. Returning to her childhood home, and then writing about that and the entire episode with Larry, enabled her to connect on a much deeper level to her own psychological reality, and to be accepting of it.

## The Social Function of Stories

Life storytelling is an act of affirming and validating our own experience in relation to those around us. Sharing our story with others helps us understand our commonalities with others and therefore feel more connected to others. The bond established in this exchange helps us maintain a sense of community and to understand the established order around us, as we become more aware of the range of possible roles and standards that exist within the human community.

Stories clarify and maintain our place in the social order of things. They confirm our own experience through a deeper understanding of the moral, ethical, and social implications of our situation. In an era when our concept of the good life is no longer one lived in fixed adherence to fixed principles, we are again on our own to discover for ourselves how our experience and feelings fit with what we see around us. Our stories tell us that to exist is to be in process in a world made up of change, but that the more we know about our own situation, the more we are like everyone else and the more everyone is like us.

A woman wrote about an experience of her childhood that helped her understand a very important social lesson.

Once upon a time, long before television figured prominently in the lives of people, there lived an 8 year old girl in a small suburb of Chicago. It wasn't a very prosperous neighborhood but since everyone started out there, the children had nothing else to compare it to. So no one felt deprived and most were content, except Vicky. It's not that she longed for material things, she longed rather for the safety and security that other kids seemed to have. Vicky was just plain tired of being made to feel unworthy. You see, she never experienced the niceties that sometimes go along with motherhood. Some mothers hugged and praised their children for the work they brought home from school, regardless of the grade marked on the paper. They understood that children were children and not always neat or quiet or considerate or perfect and, most of all, needed positive reinforcement to thrive. What Vicky didn't know was that just living was terribly painful for her mother. So, because her mother didn't do the "mommy things" that other mothers did, Vicky went in search for those comforts outside of her home, and the most logical place to turn was her teacher.

In the second grade, Vicky had a beautiful, young teacher named Marilyn Marozzi. She had long, blond hair, a slim, trim figure, and long shapely legs. Vicky believed her to be the perfect example of womanhood and hoped that she would look just like Mrs. Marozzi when she grew up. She so idolized her teacher that she hung on her every word and did very well under her tutelage. As the school year approached its end, Mrs. Marozzi decided to hold a championship spelling bee. She had been charting all of the students' spelling test scores since they had returned from Christmas vacation. For every perfect test score, a gold star was placed next to the deserving student's name on a large chart hanging on the bulletin board. If Vicky had known the test scores would be used to qualify for the spelling bee, she would not have taken the tests so lightly. She did not have enough gold stars to qualify for the competition.

Vicky was very disappointed that she would not be included in the elite group of students who would be competing for the blue ribbon. To be recognized by her peers and her beloved Mrs. Marozzi as someone special was important. It was this need to be acknowledged and accepted that drove her to cheat. One afternoon, Vicky volunteered to stay after school to clean the backboard. Though Mrs. Marozzi had a meeting to attend, she trusted one of her star pupils to stay after school, unsupervised. It proved to be too much of a temptation and Vicky removed the gold stars from her teacher's desk and placed enough next to her name to ensure a place in the competition. She had not premeditated the act, it just happened. But in cheating, she had set up a roller coaster of unexpected emotions.

It had been excrutiating to keep her secret from her best friend Mindy. But as the day of the spelling bee approached, Vicky could barely contain her excitement. As the five contestants stood before the class doing battle against the onslaught of spelling words, the pitch of suspense increased. One by one, the students fell until only Vicky and one other student remained. It was at this moment that Vicky realized she may indeed win and instead of wielding the fatal blow, she choked on a word that not only she, but the entire class knew how to spell. Somewhere deep within her soul, she knew that she was not entitled to be competing and therefore not entitled to go home with the prize. She did go home with the second place ribbon but to her surprise, her victory felt empty. Instead of being touched with each word of praise, she winced with guilt. It was an achievement to the world outside, but inside she knew she was living a lie.

The story does not end there. Vicky's deceitful actions so haunted her that she knew she had to confess all to her teacher. This was made a little more complicated by the fact that Vicky feared the loss of Mrs. Marozzi's approval. School had been Vicky's refuge. It had been a place where she received praise for accomplishments, encouragement to try again, and appreciation for just being herself. The thought of losing all of that made her hesitate. But she had become so uncomfortable with her guilt that she decided to trust Mrs. Marozzi with her confession. And she was not to be disappointed. Though Mrs. Marozzi was disappointed in Vicky for cheating and made her return the second place ribbon, she was also proud of Vicky for coming forward with the truth. And so, Vicky learned a valuable lesson about truth telling that spring. That it is much more uncomfortable and far less rewarding to live a lie, than it is to stand in your own truth.

Knowing the truth, and living according to it, creates a firm foundation for living an integrated, meaningful life. The act of going with our own truth not only takes us to a deeper level of psychological well-being, it also validates our own experience and allows us to feel more connected with others. Discovering this on our own can be a very powerful and "valuable lesson."

## The Mystical Function of Stories

Telling our stories is an act of transcending the personal and entering the realm of the sacred. In recognition of the diversity of our particular experiences and the unity of our common life themes, we feel a sense of awe, humility, and respect as we come face to face with an ultimate mystery that words fail to describe. Sharing our life story with others beyond our immediate ties links us to the circle of life that crosses time and culture.

Stories thus serve to awaken a feeling of wonder and reverence toward life. They take us beyond the here and now, beyond our everyday existence, and allow us to enter the domain where all life is sacred. Whatever we emphasize the most in our stories shows us what is most important to us, what our greatest struggles are, what our greatest triumphs are, where our deepest values lie. Our stories tell us what our potential is, what we most want to do to help others. They show us what our quest has been, where we have been broken, where we are whole, and where we are most authentically us. This is where we come in contact with the holy, the eternal, the spiritual, in all life and in our own. Stories connect us to the soul of life, to its depths and to its heights. Stories may show us a living hell, but they also show us how it is humanly possible to create heaven within us and around us. Stories give us—sometimes in a flash—profound insights or gems of wisdom beyond our years or experience. And for whatever this new understanding of life brings us, we are forever grateful. Stories remind us of the sacredness of all life. To tell our life story is to tell our spiritual autobiography.

I am particularly moved by the experience of the seventy-year old widow in my class who met her husband when they were both in pre-med school. She gave up her own plans to become a medical doctor and supported her husband in his medical career while raising three daughters. In the two years following her husband's death, she earned a master's degree in adult education and gerontology and did much journal writing, along with the intensive autobiographical and personal mythmaking work of the class. Here are her reflections on the entire process of writing about her life:

> This has been a journey into the unknown, into the depths and heights of my being. This was the way my life unfolded, with its own pattern, uniquely mine, and I am content. I would not change a single winding of the path, nor any road not taken. I would dare not, for if I had made one alteration in the tide of affairs, the voyage of my life might have been "bound in shallows and in miseries."
>
> My mother gave me the desire to fulfill my greatest potential. I cannot say whether I have; I can only say I have tried. I have come to grips with the submergence of this goal for many years in my conflicting need for the nurturing role in marriage and in motherhood, fostered by the prevailing archetype of my generation of women, and countless generations before mine. I have realized that it was not my dilemma alone, but a result of the Judeo-Christian patriarchal society, from which few women could break the fetters until the recent emergence of the Feminist Movement, too late for this aspect of my life. And I sometimes pity my daughters, caught in the dilemma of their own times.
>
> I have been the Earth Mother, attempting to be all things to all people. I have been Minerva, or Athena, although I was never "my father's daughter," but my mother's. And finally I am me, to mine own self true. I can do no more. But the journey is not yet over, and the journey is more important than the goal. I shall continue striving until my last breath. Only then can I say, "It was a life well lived!"

She completed her master's degree exactly fifty years after her undergraduate degree and has been doing grief counseling and life review work with her peers. In the process of writing about her life, she found a new degree of respect for the mystery of her own life. She found the holy in her life, and she listened to the voice of her soul. Recently, she decided that her work could best be accomplished by getting her divinity degree and becoming ordained. She has pulled a strong thread in her life, buried for many years, back to the surface, revealing a powerful and determined "will within."

## The Cosmological Function of Stories

Telling our stories is an act of bringing order to our universe by making it clearer to us how we see the world, the universe around us, and our role and place within it. The lives we live and the stories we tell about them each present an image of the world and the universe of which we are a part. Our individual world view speaks through the story we tell about our life. Science and religion, fact and faith, merge in our life stories to produce a personal perspective of how our life fits together with all other life in the universe. Our life story can also present an ideal view of the way we would like the world to look.

Stories give us a sharper picture of what our role in the world might be. We have it quite different today than Columbus or Magellan, Copernicus or Galileo, had it in their time. Today, there are fewer frontiers to conquer, fewer chances of coming up with an inaccurate picture of the universe. In fact, our image and knowledge of the universe is pretty clear. Phrases we hear more and more of these days include "global village," "world economy," "new world order."

The question today is, how do our lives, our stories, fit with these new images of our world? The stories we tell about our own lives should sometimes help us to see how our life fits together with everything else—as Schopenhauer says, like one big symphony.[3] Knowing our life this intimately, being aware of our own truths and strong threads, how they all fit together, and how our story fits with all other stories, fulfills the cosmological function of stories. The stories we tell today need to make sense in the world we live in today. I have a little story of my own that helped me make sense of our world today.

> One time, when I was a teacher on a school ship in a semester-at-sea program on a Norwegian square-rigger that had about fifty high school students, ten teachers, and thirty Norwegian crew members, we were sailing from Dakar, Senegal back to Norway, and we stopped at the Azores where I took a small group of students on a field trip to an isolated village that was actually inside a long extinct volcanic crater. It was a beautiful setting, twin lakes, one blue and the other green, with an atmosphere that I imagined came right from the eighteenth century. We caught the only bus going to the village that day, and immediately a Portuguese man started up a conversation with us that we could not understand. We knew, though, that he was being friendly and trying to tell us something that he thought was important. We arrived at the village in the middle of a festive celebration. A procession of horse-drawn carts and wagons was being led through the streets. We felt quite out

of place, like maybe we were intruding on something. We began to wonder whether we should just go off by ourselves and explore another part of the village. But soon we were called over to one of the homes. Before we knew it, we were taken in like long-lost cousins and offered some of the homemade cheese and bread that was being distributed to all the homes for the celebration of the Feast Day. We were soon humbled by the overwhelming hospitality and generosity we received from them.

Later, on the same trip, after the school year was over and the ship was docked in Bergen, I traveled on to the land of the midnight sun. One night, I rolled out my sleeping bag and went to sleep in a quiet field. Early the next morning, I awoke with goats grazing beside me. When I looked up some more, I noticed a farmer coming toward me. My first thought was, "I'm in his pasture, and he's going to kick me off." I began to feel like a trespasser. As he got closer I noticed a bit of a smile on his face. Before I knew it, he was inviting me to his home for breakfast. I still felt a little uneasy, but I followed him and found that his wife had already prepared a hearty, delicious Norwegian breakfast for me. Again, I felt totally humbled by their warm hospitality. They made it possible for me to feel part of their family, and also part of the human family.

Each time I recall these experiences or tell these stories, I am reminded that my world view changed dramatically on those two days. I began to feel like I was at home wherever I happened to be. These experiences gave me a completely new perspective on everything, they enabled me to know what it means to feel like a world citizen.

## WHY WE TELL OUR STORIES

Becoming more reflective of the things that happen to us can lead to developing the art of telling stories about our lives. Self-reflection enhances and expands our experience. It can add greater meaning to the experience we have already had. Reflection and introspection help us put events and feelings in order. The more we reflect on what has happened, or how we feel, the clearer it all becomes. The clearer our experiences and feelings are, the more we will want to share them with others.

Telling the stories of our own lives enhances our experiences, and gives them greater meaning. By putting our thoughts about ourselves down on paper, we give words to thoughts that might not have had words before. When they exist only in our minds, thoughts can be pretty vague. Written, or spoken, thoughts are usually clearer and more specific. As storytellers, we seek—and find—deeper meaning in what we thought we knew before, but didn't really know we didn't know until we expressed it with words. Writing—giving real words to our thoughts—brings clarity, and clarity— understanding what we have said about ourselves—brings self-knowledge, while self-knowledge brings meaning. The more meaning we find in life, the more we get out of life.

Telling our story, and sharing the meaning we find in our own life, also helps to connect us more to the human community. By sharing our story, we find that we have a lot more in common with others than we might have thought. This sharing of stories creates a bond between people who may not even have known each other before. After sharing, or listening to, a life story, a connection is established that remains even if we don't see the other person again.

Telling stories about our experience also helps to clarify our sense of a personal identity. The telling of our experience to others brings it into a sharper focus for us, and we end up with an even stronger sense of who we are and what we have become. Both our self-image and self-esteem gain in clarity and strength when we tell our story.

We may also tell our stories as a way of purging or releasing ourselves of certain burdens. We may not even be aware that part of the story we carry within us is a burden to us until we let it go and let another person hear it. Telling our stories can therefore be an important way of validating our own experience of life. When we tell a part of our story to another, and it is not taken as something totally weird but as something that another person can understand, relate to, and accept, we realize that we are not so unusual as we might have thought we were. Our own particular story is then seen as legitimate, as something that is valid and has its own value. We then discover that our experience is actually similar to that of other people.

We may even discover in telling parts of our story that feel a little strange or uncomfortable to us that we "stretch" or "invent" the truth[4] of our story a bit to make it fit our own image of ourselves, and in so doing we find out what the personal and social bounds are within which our story will be accepted and believed by others.

However, for some, telling a truthful life story is a risk that is essential to the process itself. For example, those in twelve-step recovery programs find that not only is telling their story a very powerful part of their recovery, but that they also are expected to tell their story as part of the treatment program. What they find out is that their recovery may not be complete or successful unless they can get beyond denial and tell their story as it actually happened. When this is done, everyone in the group recognizes the truth of the story being told because it fits with their experience, too. A truthful story is the most validating story of all. A truthful story is what really connects us all to each other, because it fits best of all. Telling a truthful life story takes an enormous load off our hearts.

These are all natural parts of the life storytelling process. Not the least of the reasons why we tell life stories is that we want to be entertaining; we like to be entertained. To tell a life story in a way that not only creates a real human link with others but also makes another laugh, or even cry, that is perhaps entertainment at its best, and certainly life storytelling at its best.

It is an equally valid reason to tell our life story because we want to be acknowledged. There are a great many of us who are not famous or well known and who therefore may not be able to let the "public" know who we are and what we have done through the telling of our life story in book form, but who nevertheless want to, and should, tell our story to others through whatever means is available.

Everyone's life story is meaningful, full of sacred elements, valid, valuable, linked to all others, and entertaining. To want to tell our story is to want to be part of the human family. We tell our life stories because they are a part of us. The stories we tell about ourselves attempt to define our lives, give them order, and put them in a perspective that makes sense to us. Our stories identify the influences that made us who we are today, help us to see ourselves better and, ultimately, to accept ourselves more. The important thing in telling our stories is to remember that out of the conflict comes its resolution. The particular circumstances of our lives may not matter as much as how we see them. A change of perception can come at any time we are ready to accept what has happened to us as okay. The only thing we can change about our past is the way we look at it. This can be a creative response that enables us to understand the flow of our lives and to accept it.

Telling our stories may be the most important way we have of giving our lives meaning, healing those parts of our lives that need it, making peace with ourselves, and gaining the power from stories that they have for us. Through telling our stories we can experience many forms of release, recovery, resolution, or renewal.

Knowing our story well helps us to know ourselves, others, the mystery of life, and the universe around us better than we had before. It has been said that our ability to see our life as a comprehensible story is a key to our own happiness.[5] Life stories make up the thread that connects the human family. It may well be that we can leave no greater legacy than the story of our life.

In the chapters that follow, we will explore these many levels of the transformation process that begins with greater self-awareness from giving yourself the gift of your own story, and that reaches its culmination in gaining a clearer sense of our full role in life and in the world and in giving the power of stories to others.

## NOTES

1. Coles, *The call of stories*, pp 204–205.
2. Campbell, *The masks of God*, pp. 609–624.
3. Quoted by Campbell, *The power of myth*, p. 229.

4. Zinsser (ed.), *Inventing the truth.*
5. Kotre and Hall, *Seasons of life.*

# 2

# *Recognizing the Enduring Elements of Sacred Stories*

> Storytelling is fundamental to the human search for meaning, whether we tell tales of the creation of the earth or of our own early choices.[1]

One of the stories of the first stories ever told, about how storytelling came to be, is from the Seneca people.

In a long ago time, there was a boy who hunted every day in the forest. One day, he sat down next to a large stone to fix his bow and arrows.

He heard a voice speak to him, saying, "I will tell you a story."

The boy was surprised and a little afraid because there was no one around. He looked all around the stone, and finally decided it could only be the stone. He thought the stone must have orenda, the magic power the old men talk about. So he spoke to it. "What did you say you wanted to tell me?"

"They are called stories; they are traditions. But first you must give me a present for telling it to you."

The boy offered up the partridge he had just caught, and placed it on the stone. "Come back later tonight," said the stone, "and I will tell you a legend about the world that was."

The boy came back that evening, sat on the stone, and the voice told him the story of the people who lived in the sky above, the first people, the ones with great magic. By the time the story was over, the boy had dozed off. Then the voice said, "Tell me if you become sleepy, and we can rest. If you sleep you will not hear. Come back tomorrow evening, and I will tell you more. Remember to bring my present."

The next evening, after his hunting, the boy came back to the stone and offered it some more birds. This time he listened to the story without missing a word. He returned the next night, and the one after that.

One day, when they were out hunting, his friend asked him where he disappeared to at night. "I go to hear stories," he replied. "What are they?" Since he could not tell his friend about them, he said, "Come with me tonight and you will hear for yourself."

So they went and heard more stories. Stories of the stone coats, the flying heads, the porcupine people. Soon the whole village heard the news of the stone and its stories. Then the whole tribe came and listened, bearing gifts of fresh game. They marveled over the things called stories that came from the stone. Tales about "The Master of Life," "He Who Is Our Grandfather," and many others. They understood that great wisdom came from the stone. It took four years for the stone to tell all its tales, but the nights passed quickly.

One evening, after it had told the last story, and after all the others had left, the stone said to the boy, "One day you will become old and unable to hunt. These stories will help you in your old age. Tell these tales to others, but make sure that they give you something in return for them."

The boy grew old and did not forget the stories. He told them to anyone who came to his lodge to listen. Travelers from faraway tribes came to hear the stories and gladly gave him gifts. There were few nights when his lodge did not have a crowd of listeners, enthralled with the stories he told.[2]

This story of "The Storytelling Stone" is one version of how stories came to be, how they were passed on, and how they got their magic power that captures our imagination, even today. The story still charms us because it expresses in the way only a story can the timeless qualities of reciprocity and right relation to the earth. These are important values to keep alive, and this is accomplished through passing the stories from one generation to another. The story also expresses these values in a familiar and recognizable form. This, too, helps keep them alive. In fact, among American Indians, when children did wrong, the power of storytelling was used to show the right way; the power of the stories was usually enough!

Stories are what held the community of the past together. Traditional stories, told orally, contained within them the history, social laws, spiritual truths, and cultural values of families and their communities. We continue to pass stories along, year after year, generation after generation, because their timeless elements possess an intrigue, a power, and an ability to transform our lives. Today, stories retain their power because we tell them in essentially the same form as we always have; we continue to pass along our most cherished truths in stories, as well.

Storytelling has always been a fundamental form for expressing meaning in life. The earliest myths and legends explained the mysteries of the world, or some part of them, to their listeners. These stories were told and retold, over and over, because they contained the important knowledge and wisdom that had to be learned by each generation. They originated as sacred stories and became traditional stories, passed on orally.

Memory is the mother of culture.[3] Memory, and the need to remember wisdom, is what kept these sacred stories alive. Each time a story was told from memory, culture was reborn and renewed. One aspect that helped make it possible to remember all the stories, and the important wisdom they carried, was that sacred stories repeated within them certain elements that also made understanding them a little easier. Traditional stories repeat patterns, themes, and motifs that become familiar to storytellers as well as to listeners because they represent some of the events, experiences, and emotions shared by all human beings. They are aspects of life common to everyone. They represent a truth of human life.

Traditional stories are sacred stories for many reasons. Not only do they carry within them the common elements of the human experience and the most vital values for maintaining community life, but they also do this in a form that is highly familiar to all storytellers and listeners. Even more important, they are sacred because they provide us with a part of our collective experience as members of the human race. They carry images that are ever present around us and images of experiences that are repeated over and over within us—images from the natural world (mountains, seas, deserts, the sky), images from the psychological world (birth, struggle, love, death)—because these images are central to our well-being. They are sacred because they carry the images that connect us to our ultimate concerns, to our essential humanness. They carry a power that we intuitively respond to from the core of our being because they show us what we are capable of when we live fully and deeply.

Sacred stories convey that part of life that is most vital to our maintaining and passing on the cultural truths that sustain society. We sometimes have to read between the lines, or even have a similar experience of our own, to recognize that they speak a universal language. When we do connect with a story through our own experience of the event or through the feeling being described in the story, we are also connected to others by means of the story having articulated our common experience. One of the reasons this is possible is that it is all done in a form that is recognizable to all: a beginning, a middle, and an end always tie them together.

Myth is perhaps the most familiar—and important—form of sacred story.[4] A myth is a metaphorical and symbolic story that conveys the deepest truth about life and that at the same time captures the universal aspects of being human. Understanding the symbolic meaning of what is represented in myths can assist our own psychological and spiritual development. The process of transformation that Inanna, Gilgamesh, Isis, Odysseus, and all other mythic figures go through demonstrates practical applications of the universal pattern that can help us understand our own transformations in life.

What is most important about myth, in the classic sense, is that it is really the opposite of what is thought of in the popular sense. Rather than being seen as a falsehood, myth is traditionally accepted as representing what is most true about human life on an inner level, even though outwardly the story may appear unbelievable. One of the better definitions of myth is that offered by a child who said, "A myth is a story that is make believe on the outside, but true on the inside."

## THE ENDURING ELEMENTS

What do the Biblical story of Job, the myth of Odysseus, and the fairy tale of Sleeping Beauty have in common? Each story, and all other traditional stories, shares certain elements that are timeless and universal and therefore extremely relevant to the lives and circumstances of every human being. These stories follow a recognizable script, or form (a beginning, a middle, and an end) through which they express a truth, a wisdom, certain values, or a lesson of life. The form dresses up the story line so that its lesson, or truth, comes across in a familiar and entertaining fashion. Sacred stories come in a form that conveys an ultimate reality or way of viewing the world. They carry meaning for both the person and the community as a whole.

Specifically, these stories have in common the timeless elements of *metaphor* and *symbol*, *archetype* and *motif*, *pattern* and *repetition*. Each one helps make the stories more interesting, exciting, and powerful. They are what give stories their magic and help them endure generation after generation.

In the biblical story of Job, for example, there is great suffering followed by redemption. Job is a good man with a good family who is tested to his limits by God. First, he loses his servants and his children at the hands of the Chaldean troops. Then his friends say he must have done something evil to deserve such a fate. But Job insists that his deeds have been good. Then God answers him out of a whirlwind, and bids him to array himself "with glory and beauty" to show his faith. Job ultimately proves himself courageous and patient before an even worse fate. He says, "I have heard of thee by the hearing of the ear: but now mine eye seeth thee" (Job 42:5). And, overcoming his ordeal with an abiding faith, Job is rewarded with a new house, new servants, new sons and daughters, and 140 years!

In the Greek myth, *The Odyssey*, Odysseus and his army have conquered Troy, yet their homeward journey is more challenging than their recent battles. Winds rip the sails of the ship to shreds and carry them helpless for nine days until they come to the land of the Lotus Eaters, where his men take a drug of forgetfulness and lose their desire to return home. Odysseus drags them back on board, ties them to the ship, and sets sail again, only to encounter the Cyclops, the one-eyed ogre who captures them in his cave. They escape, but are blown backward, then some of the crew are cannibalized, and later the remainder are temporarily transformed into swine. Then Odysseus is guided through an underworld night-sea adventure to Hades, where he learns the balance between male and female and the way of the safe passage home. However, his last ship is wrecked and he alone saved. He washes ashore on the island of Calypso and lives with the beautiful goddess for eight years in an idyllic setting, yet often gazes out to sea, homeward, for his Penelope. Only after the last leg of his eighteen-year return journey, which is spent in deep sleep on a magic ship, is he fully prepared to return home and resume his life as a considerate spouse and father.

In the German folk tale, *Sleeping Beauty*,[5] a king and queen get their wish to have a child, "a girl so beautiful that the king was beside himself with joy and ordered a great feast." There are thirteen Wise Women in the kingdom, but only twelve are invited. The child receives magic gifts from the Wise Women—virtue, beauty, wealth, all the desirable things in the world. But the thirteenth appears anyway and places a vengeful spell upon the child: in her fifteenth year she will be pricked by a spindle and fall down dead. The twelfth Wise Woman, who has yet to offer her gift, can only modify the spell and say the princess will fall into a deep sleep that will last 100 years. And that is what happens, even though the king tries to prevent it. The princess, the king, the queen, and the royal household all are under the spell. After exactly 100 years, a prince comes along and awakens her with a kiss, not because he is a prince but simply because it is the right time. Then, the whole household awakens, and a splendid wedding is celebrated. Each of these timeless elements has its particular role in traditional stories.

## Metaphor and Symbol

A *metaphor* conveys an important message through the mask of comparison.[6] The comparison connects two previously unconnected ideas and gives a new and much greater meaning to the term being amplified. A metaphor takes us by surprise and tells us something we hadn't thought of before.

A metaphor is using one term that is fairly well understood to help explain another term that we want to be understood in a new or different way: "Earth is woman." Many meanings and images can be evoked from this metaphor. First, we think of the earth as living and as nurturing. Then, we think of the earth in all her beauty, with shapes and forms like mountains and valleys. Then, we may think of her water as the water (or blood) of life. And when we begin to see her with the eyes of respect and honor, she becomes sacred, too.

Metaphors from the natural world around us are probably the most common comparisons to our own lives. We often hear life compared to a tree, a river, a mountain, the cycle of the seasons, or a path. These are all metaphors that have a quality that helps us understand some aspect of our own lives better. These images, when applied to life, give life a certain order and structure that we might have overlooked before.

Metaphors use the language of the imagination. They enable a new way of seeing, and add a new dimension to, a term we might not otherwise think of in that light. A metaphor livens up any text or narrative and gives it a richer feeling. Myth is often expressed in metaphors, and that is one of the reasons why myths carry such power for us. A wonderful way to enliven our own stories is to speak metaphorically, if it happens naturally.

In the story of Job, the overall metaphor is the use of suffering (including pain, loss, hardship) to represent the way we develop spiritually. If we understand the function of the suffering Job endured, we understand the process of spiritual growth. In *The Odyssey*, a difficult journey is used as a metaphor in the same way, for the same purpose, to help us understand spiritual development. And in *Sleeping Beauty*, a long sleep is used to represent the process of transformation.

A *symbol* is a sign, object, or thing that binds together two usually very different terms.[7] The term being used as the symbol carries a dual meaning. Its common meaning is well known, but its symbolic meaning is often hidden and even more profound. When we say, "The dove is a symbol of peace," we are actually saying the dove represents peace or carries a hidden meaning of peace. The dove, used as a symbol, carries both its common meaning (bird) and its hidden meaning (peace). Even though the dove is fairly common as a symbol, there are some who may only think of it as a bird, while others will think of peace immediately upon seeing a dove.

When we are able to think symbolically, our understanding of what is being said is enhanced tremendously. Deeper levels of meaning are opened to us that would otherwise remain closed. Bringing symbols into the telling of our own life stories is likely to contribute to our own integration.

Sacred stories speak the language of symbolism, too. When Job says, "Mine eye seeth thee," we can take that literally or symbolically. In the latter case, it would mean that he now has true spiritual knowledge of God. Odysseus's entire journey can also be understood literally or symbolically. On a symbolic level, all the external difficulties he encounters could signify the character transformation and spiritual awakening he is experiencing internally. Sleeping Beauty's 100-year sleep can be seen as a symbolic representation of the 100 days of winter, when the earth lies in dormant sleep before its spring rebirth, as the time when the curse is naturally up, or as symbolic of the time necessary for her to come of age. In each case, the process of inner transformation has been portrayed with different outer circumstances.

## Archetype and Motif

An *archetype* is the mold from which all other things of the same type are made.[8] It is a pattern in its original form, an original idea from which all other related ideas are derived. The Greeks believed that original ideas were in the minds of the gods and therefore preceded experience. As time and experience expanded, each archetype took on many new variations, depending on how people in different settings or circumstances experienced the idea. One archetype, therefore, acquired many forms. An example is the archetype of birth, an experience common to all human beings, that has acquired numerous variations based on the many possible social or cultural ways of experiencing it.

An archetype is a major element of our common human experience. A *motif* is a minor element, or smaller part, of our common experience. Both recur often in our lives and are also predictable, because they are the essence of the human experience. We can be sure that what is essential, and central to our existence, will come around again and again. The predictability of archetypes and motifs being repeated in our lives is what gives them their power over us and makes them fascinating to us.

Archetypes express the inherited, or latent, potentialities of the human psyche. They are the vast store of our ancestral knowledge about our relationship to God and the world around us. When pieces of this knowledge come up to our conscious level of awareness—whether from direct experience, a dream, or through a traditional story—and we are able to integrate the meaning of the experience into our lives, we are drawn into a universal and eternal process that connects us to the experience of all who have gone before us and all who will come after us. Archetypes that emerge in our lives in this way become a kind of "personal mythology" and present an impressive parallel to the great traditional mythologies of all people and epochs. (How we can recognize and understand the role of these timeless elements of the human experience in our own lives today, and use their benefits, are the topics of chapters 4, 6, and 7.)

There are literally thousands of archetypes.[9] The inner-world archetypes include the ego, the persona, the shadow, and the anima and animus. Family members can also be archetypal figures: mother, father, son, daughter, grandmother, grandfather, sister, brother, twins, orphans. Phases of the life cycle can also be archetypal: child, puer, senex, crone; as can various roles we play: hero, victim, trickster, shaman, healer, invalid, friend.

One of the most familiar archetypes is that of the hero. The first major element of the hero story is the separation from the familiar, or the call to adventure, which is also an archetype. Job, Odysseus, and Sleeping Beauty are each archetypal heroes/heroines. They each receive a call to adventure that ultimately transforms them into someone they weren't before they received the call.

Another familiar archetype is that of death and rebirth. Again, in quite different ways, each of the three stories expresses this archetype. Through his extensive suffering, Job's faith is tested to its limit only to be renewed and emerge even stronger. Not only do Odysseus's rough edges die away through his extended ordeals, but he is also reborn inwardly to be a more fitting husband and father when he returns. And Sleeping Beauty is reborn from an extended sleep, ready to begin a new life. Transformation is the central theme, or archetype, of all three stories.

### Pattern and Repetition

A *pattern* is a design, model, or plan that is repeated over and over again. A pattern is a regular, predictable way of doing something. Traditional, socially prescribed rites of passage all follow the same predictable three-phase pattern of separation-initiation-return or birth-death-rebirth.[10]

If memory is the mother of culture, *repetition* is the midwife to culture. Repetition is an aid to our memory, to the way we remember things. It is also the way important things in life are driven home to us. Repetition helps us understand important patterns. The cycle of the seasons conveys the essential lesson of birth, death, and rebirth. The annual repetition of spring, summer, fall, and winter is both a metaphor and a symbol of the pattern of birth, death, and rebirth.[11]

Sacred stories use repetition to present us with a familiar pattern, or story line, over and over. A particular theme, or motif, may recur frequently in many different stories, yet no story is exactly the same as another. There is always some new twist or variation from one story to the next. Stories give us a structure, but also show us that the protagonist's actions and reactions are due as much to choice as they are to circumstance.

Stories everywhere are known for their universal pattern of having a beginning, a middle, and an end. But what we learn first from sacred stories, whether myth or folk tale, is that every story also has a beginning, a muddle, and a resolution.[12] A muddle is when things don't go smoothly. It is when things involve conflict, chaos, or disorder. Conflict creates the plot of a story. There could be no plot, plan of action, intrigue, or drama to the story, without a muddle of some sort. Stories go from order to disorder to order. This is the pattern that is repeated over and over. (This "sacred pattern" is discussed in more detail in chapter 3.)

Our three stories not only follow the pattern of having a clear beginning, conflict, and resolution but also have their own particular ways in which repetition is important. Job's conflict is all the suffering he has to endure, not once, but many times. Odysseus's muddle is facing and overcoming one difficult situation after another on his return home. And Sleeping Beauty receives not one but twelve gifts (virtues) from the Wise Women, but a thirteenth puts her in the muddle of the story until it is time to awaken.

Nor is Sleeping Beauty the only one to fall into a deep sleep: everyone in the royal household does, "right down to the flies on the wall," to emphasize the symbolic importance of the sleep.

These are the predictably repeated and enduring elements found in all forms of sacred stories. They live on across time and culture because generations of storytellers have found them to be the most satisfying and meaningful ways to express the essence of the human experience. What metaphor, symbol, archetype, and pattern really do is guide our spiritual development when we consciously understand how they play a role in our own lives. All the great spiritual and religious teachers of the world have used these enduring elements as a way of passing on their spiritual truth. When the disciples asked Jesus why he spoke to them in parables, he said because that is way the mysteries of heaven are known (Matt. 13:10–23).

We are recognizing again today that stories help us see the important truths in everyday experience. This is why we are now seeing a renewal of interest in storytelling. Sacred stories help us see the pattern, the meaning, and the purpose in our own lives. Children learn from them that the struggle against great odds is part of life, that those struggles can be overcome by facing them head on, and that in the end we can emerge victorious. This is the pattern of beginning, conflict, and resolution that is repeated again and again in every story.

Sacred stories, and the timeless elements they contain, mirror our own life situations today. We can recognize our own predicaments or dreams in them. They become models for our own lives. We can reproduce the solutions they offer in our own conflict situations. They provide us with a message or image that we can store away and later pull out to use when we most need it. The virtues of archetypal figures, like the faith, courage, and persistence of both Job and Odysseus, can serve us well at any point when we might need those qualities to get ourselves out of a confusing or difficult situation.

The timeless motifs and archetypes that recur in the world's traditional literature show us that there are many experiences that have been experienced by others before us. The more aware of, and familiar with, these enduring elements we are, the more will the stories we tell about our lives connect with those others tell about themselves.

The new openness to story and myth is a sign of our renewed interest in the essence of the human experience. I believe our desire to tell the stories of our lives is also a way to rediscover our spiritual essence. Through thinking and writing autobiographically; through moving from our unique experiences to a recognition of our common experiences with others; through seeing, understanding, and embracing our entire life experience and identifying the strong threads and central theme of our lives; we may come to accept and rejoice in the beings we are.

Our challenge is to make the stories we tell about ourselves once again sacred. We owe it to ourselves to give our own lives as much respect and reverence as we once gave the lives of the gods and goddesses.

## NOTES

1. Bateson, *Composing a life*, p. 34.

2. *Parabola*, 4(4): pp. 12–14. Retold by John Cech, "The Story Telling Stone." *Parabola*.

3. Csikszentmihalyi, *Flow*, pp. 120–24.

4. See Eliade, *Myth and reality*; and Campbell, *The power of myth*.

5. The Grimm Brothers' (1968) tale, "Sleeping Beauty," is also called "Briar rose," pp. 186–191

6. See Edwards, *The storyteller's goddess*, p. 5; and Rico, *Writing the natural way*, ch. 9.

7. See Jacobi, *Complex archetype symbol*.

8. See Jacobi, *Complex archetype symbol*; and Jung, *The archetypes and the collective unconscious*.

9. See Downing, *Mirrors of the self*.

10. Eliade, *The myth of the eternal return*.

11. Ibid.

12. The idea for the beginning-muddle-resolution form of the pattern came from many sources, especially Bateson, *Steps to an ecology of mind*; and Tolkien, *Tree and leaf*.

# 3

## *Seeing Our Own Stories as Sacred*

Wholeness is always relative and gives us something to work on as long as we live.[1]

In biology, physical development is considered to be governed by the genome, or the entire genetic program of the species. Another principle in biology (homeorhesis[2]) says we persist along the specific pathway or course of our biological development once we have started out on it despite the environmental variations we encounter. Thus, our biological development is meant to unfold according to an innate program, or blueprint, while we also have an inborn tendency that keeps us on our own biological path in order to fulfill that blueprint, despite complications that would throw us off course.

What if we thought of psychological and spiritual development in this way? Could we find a similar inborn program, or blueprint, meant to guide the psychospiritual development of our entire species? If there were such a psychospiritual blueprint for our lives, discovering that blueprint, and recognizing our lives as having unfolded according to its pattern, would make our lives, and the story we tell about our lives, sacred, simply because the blueprint for our psychospiritual development would be sacred. If we could discover the way things are meant to be, the way we were designed to live, and what we are to learn from living that way, then we could think of living by the blueprint as living in a sacred manner.

There may be such a blueprint for psychological and spiritual transformation in the sacred pattern of stories. The pattern is like the genome within us, and living the pattern is like homeorhesis, or what enables us to stay on the course we are meant to be on. The pattern, like an archetype, is an original form that is repeated over and over in our lives and assists our psychological development because it is an inborn psychological program we have been designed to understand. Because the pattern follows the same three steps of beginning, muddle, and resolution each time it comes into our lives, it helps us maintain the psychological trajectory we are on despite the hurdles that are thrown in our way.

To illustrate, we can see this pattern, this blueprint, in operation most clearly in the thousands of traditional stories that have been told and retold for generations throughout our history. In fact, these stories—myths, folktales, and legends—have been kept alive across countless generations not only because they contain timeless truths and values about right living but also because they are all told in the same basic form of this three-part pattern. It is precisely this form that is meant to facilitate development and transformation. The pattern these traditional stories follow illustrates every time that we not only continue to maintain a balance between opposing forces in our lives, as in homeostasis, but that we also overcome difficult situations that arise and forge ahead with our growth as a homeorhesis. This pattern of birth-death-rebirth tells us that we have a natural tendency to find our way to those experiences in life that will lead us through our own transformation.

The pattern has many versions, as seen in Exhibit 3.1. An example of both the pattern and homeorhesis is given by Joseph Campbell when he describes the predicament of baby sea turtles.[3] The sea turtle lays her eggs in the sand some thirty feet or so from the water. Days later, a little multitude of tiny turtles, each about as big as a nickel, emerge and without hesitation start for the sea. No hunting around. No trial and error. Not a single one goes the wrong way. Meanwhile, a flock of seagulls comes zooming down on them like dive bombers, but the turtles keep on going right on into the water, and they already know how to swim! But as soon as they get there, the fish begin coming at them.

Life is tough, but the existence of this timeless pattern ensures that, despite difficulties, we will persist in the psychologically programmed way in order to continue to grow. It helps us move from one state of being, or status—even though we may be stuck or comfortable there—to another. And as the pattern completes itself, it can begin all over again. Becoming conscious of the pattern is what enables us to recognize it each new time it comes into our lives, and to become transformed by it. Our stories are blueprints of what is humanly possible.

The stories within us all contain the same timeless elements as sacred stories. Our life experiences are full of such elements, and can be expressed metaphorically, symbolically, archetypally, and in a form familiar to all. Our life stories, like sacred stories, have their own beginnings, muddles, and

Exhibit 3.1
The Sacred Pattern: Metaphors of Transformation—One Story, Many Versions

| | 1 | 2 | 3 |
|---|---|---|---|
| Story: | beginning (beginning) | middle (muddle) | end (resolution) |
| Ritual: (van Gennep) | separation | transition | incorporation |
| Myth: (Eliade) | birth | death | rebirth |
| (Campbell) | departure | initiation | return |
| Mysticism: (Underhill) | purification | illumination | union |
| Dialectics: | thesis | antithesis | synthesis |
| Education: | seeking knowledge | finding knowledge | applying knowledge |
| Development: | dependence (childhood) | independence (adolescence) | interdependence (adulthood) |
| Individuation: (Jung) | birth of ego | death of ego | birth of whole self |
| Transition: (Bridges) | ending | neutral zone | new beginning |
| 12 Step Programs: (A.A., etc.) | admitting powerlessness (surrender) | spiritual awakening (working the program) | recovery (telling others) |

resolutions, and often many repetitions of these. The muddle/conflict is the plot of our lives, or the challenge, that gives us direction, purpose, and meaning. The resolution is what we do to meet or overcome this challenge and carry out our purpose. Yet, it requires an effort on our part to give voice to all of this, to give our story a shape and a form that will convey its meaning to us and others. We need to become more familiar with this pattern.

The stories we tell of our lives are built upon a foundation of archetypal experiences. Our lives share a common pattern with the lives of the gods and goddesses. The first storytellers told about what they knew best, their own lives and the lives of those around them. The pattern their stories followed was experienced first in everyday life. It expressed an important mystery of life. Sacred stories, and our own life stories, have an ordered form and convey a specific meaning because they reflect life as it really is.

Every time we hear a story open with the familiar "Once upon a time . . . " we are being prepared to enter a timeless realm where a universal process of change is about to be unfolded before our eyes. This is where the familiar pattern of beginning-conflict-resolution takes place. Because this pattern means transformation, we can think of it as a sacred pattern.

## THE SACRED PATTERN

The pattern (see Exhibit 3.1) sacred stories follow constitutes an important part of the way we experience life cycle development. In our personal development, as in our stories, we progress from a beginning to some kind of a conflict, or at least a muddle, and then on to a resolution. The third part is where we usually gain wisdom or learn from the process.

This same pattern is also very evident in traditional rites of passage. Folk communities lived and understood life within the framework of life cycle passages. There was a different rite of passage for almost every transition in life. Traditional life meant experiencing deeply every transition in life. Everyone was very conscious of every transition undergone by each member of the community.

Each person's life in a traditional village followed a clearly defined process or pattern, as determined by the socially prescribed initiation rites and other ceremonies that guided and organized community life. Children would live with their parents for the first twelve years or so, and would then be selected, with other children of that age in the village, to undergo a puberty, or separation, rite. This process began with the child's *separation* from the family, and moved to a *transition* phase where the child was made aware of the traditional wisdom of the community while beginning to gain a sense of his or her adult role in that community. The third phase was the child's *incorporation* back into the family and community with new knowledge and in the role of a fully responsible member of that community.

Arnold van Gennep pointed out nearly 100 years ago that similar ritual occurred throughout the life course.[4] Each life transition was helped along with a traditional ritual or ceremony—whether it was birth, puberty, marriage, childbirth, or death—and followed the same three-step pattern. People of traditional communities were very accustomed to seeing their lives within the framework of separation-transition-return. These were the three most common archetypes of their experience.

As society became less traditional and less defined by the socially prescribed rites of passage, we began to lose the awareness we once had of this natural pattern. What happened then was that this pattern went underground—to our unconscious. It became a process that we were not consciously aware of but that was nevertheless there. We still have separation experiences, initiatory experiences, and renewal experiences in our everyday lives, but we are no longer as conscious of them as we once were. In communities founded upon tradition, the connection between unconscious thoughts and conscious experiences was much more explicit because of those socially prescribed rites of passage.

Today, when a universal experience bursts into our life, and we become consciously aware of it, it speaks with a power far beyond that of normal experience. This is what happens when a classic myth speaks to us today. Experiencing and understanding a sacred image, or archetype, is like claiming a space in the blueprint of life.

Myths tell us that every individual life mirrors the collective life of the whole. Some individual lives, though, express the archetypal pattern to a greater degree than others. We can't expect to experience the archetypal pattern of birth-death-rebirth[5] the way Christ did, but each of us has the chance to express it to the degree we are capable of based on our own life circumstances. We each have the potential to express this three-part archetypal pattern in a form and to a degree consistent with and appropriate to our own experience.

This is also the pattern expressed in all the world's myths. Joseph Campbell calls it the monomyth, and identifies its three parts as departure-initiation-return. This pattern makes up the universal formula of the mythological journey of the hero. As found in myth, it is a representation of how development and transformation occur in traditional settings. Campbell says, "A hero ventures forth from the world of common day into a region of supernatural wonder: fabulous forces are there encountered and a decisive victory is won: the hero comes back from this mysterious adventure with the power to bestow boons on his fellow man."[6]

This process, which has transformation at its heart, has taken many forms throughout history. Myth, ritual, and story are the earliest forms to follow this sacred pattern, but we find many other forms of this pattern in contemporary, everyday life, too.

In mysticism,[7] an awakening of the Self (usually an abrupt conversion) is experienced first on the path to spiritual consciousness, followed by purification (a state of pain and effort), then illumination (adventures of the soul), and a surrender (a mystic death, or dark night of the soul), before reaching their goal of union (or equilibrium, and service to God). A contemporary version of this might be the personal quest for truth, which involves first an independent investigation of truth; followed by confronting, struggling with, and finally accepting the truth one has found to be most in line with the reality of the time; then carrying this new understanding into action by serving others in one's chosen way.

Other contemporary, or secular, forms of the pattern have a strong developmental basis. The old idea of the dialectical process (thesis-antithesis-synthesis) can be relevant to development, as well, making it clear that wherever we happen to be in our life there is an opposite for that, and that if we experience loss after abundance, for example, there will follow a period where those two extremes will merge into a new state of being.

The way we learn things that are important to us follows three steps, as well. First, there is the seeking of knowledge, then finding, or attaining it (which may be a struggle that gives us a new status through a newly acquired degree), and finally applying, or doing something with that new knowledge once we have it, like giving it back to others in some way. These steps also provide the basis for the three questions that give our life its meaning: What do we seek in life? What have we found? How will we use it?

Development across the life cycle, in its essence, can be seen within the framework of the archetypal pattern, as well. We begin life pretty dependent upon others as children. The task of adolescence becomes one of breaking away from that state of dependence, to begin to discover truth on our own and find our own identity. This is where we often run into difficulties. We either remain too dependent or we go too far in expressing our independence. The goal of this independence is to come to full awareness of who we are at our core. Finally by adulthood, if we have achieved true independence, we begin to recognize how we cannot make it physically or spiritually completely on our own, and we acknowledge how important the interdependence of giving freely to others as well as receiving from others really is.

For Jung, "individuation" is the process through which we fully realize our inner potential. It is a continual maturing or unfolding process in which the ego is born, symbolically dies to its self, and is then reborn as a fully integrated, whole Self.[8]

Life itself is made up of transitions, and in Bridges's examination of the process all transitions follow, we can see yet another secular form of the pattern.[9] Each transition we experience signals an ending to something, followed by a neutral zone or limbo, an inbetween period before the new beginning begins.

The many twelve-step programs now experiencing tremendous growth (Alcoholics Anonymous, Al-Anon, Codependents Anonymous, among others) also follow the ageless archetypal pattern of transformation. They incorporate a natural healing formula which begins with admitting our powerlessness over our addiction or others (Step 1). "Working the Steps" means being willing to live our lives according to a series of principles that will help us undergo a process of spiritual awakening that includes a purging and cleansing (Steps 2 through 11). Recovery means actively practicing the principles daily, living the joy in this, and sharing our story and experience with others, giving freely without expecting anything in return (Step 12).

The pattern, in its essence, may be a microcosm of the life cycle, as well. It may be that the separation we all begin this pattern with is separation from self, or from our true center, in which case we seek a transformation of self in order to return to our self, or to our center. It may be then that whenever we find ourselves off center, we need to check out where we are in relation to this threefold pattern and let ourselves continue through the natural course of this transformational pattern to regain our center and go on our way.

## ONE BLUEPRINT FITS ALL

The transformational pattern exists in all cultures because it is the externalization of an imprint we carry within us as members of the human race. It is like having a constant inner guide to help us through our natural process of psychological development. The pattern means transformation; that is its reason for being. Going all the way through the threefold pattern changes us by moving us from one status of being to another. The transformation that occurs through consciously experiencing the pattern has everything to do with perspective. We experience the blueprint, or pattern, differently depending on where we are when we come into contact with the archetypal elements of the pattern.

If you experience or tell a story from the perspective of, for example, an inn, your experience of the pattern will be different from that of the traveler who arrives at the inn by way of the trail. Similarly, the story told from the perspective of the safe harbor will be different from the one told from the perspective of the ship.[10] Transformation is as much a matter of the ship finding its safe harbor as it is the safe harbor taking in its ship. Both are transformed in the process. It is the human journey to wholeness that the archetypal pattern is about.

We learn from mythology that it can be an external or internal quest that we have to go through to become renewed. The one who does go out on a quest can only do that with the help of others. Those others, who assist the seeker, become just as transformed in the process as the one who goes out. Both contribute an essential piece to the whole pattern, to the whole story. At one point in our lives we might experience the transformative function of the archetypal pattern from the perspective of the ship, another time from the safe harbor. At one point we might provide, and at another we might seek. The provider provides what the seeker seeks, and the seeker seeks what the provider provides.

Depending upon our perspective during our transformation, our story of it is going to be different. The ship may tell a different story of the transformation than the safe harbor, but they are both transformed when the ship finds its safe harbor and the safe harbor takes in its ship. One perspective is not any more important than the other.

May Sarton says there are people like wells, even though they are rarer in these days of diffusion, who are able to create a mood and an environment around them that just seems to attract others.[11] Their homes speak of intimacy and solitude, the secular equivalent of some churches, where one enters to know the spirit freed from all clutter and confusion. Some people, like wells, are able to express their whole being, even the secrets of their inner life, in their habitat, their personal environment. This is what creates "a world within" to which people are drawn, "as to a well of peace and joy."

A friend of mine, who has created such an environment around her by preparing meals in her home and having friends come over for good food and fellowship, told me a story recently about an experience she had. One night, during a snowstorm, a woman skidded off the road about a quarter mile from my friend's home. Though there were other homes closer to her car, the woman knocked on my friend's door. She was surprised, and a bit preoccupied with a meeting that was going on in her home, but she decided to do what she could to help the woman anyway. Before long, they had her car unstuck; but in the process their meeting became a magical encounter. Somehow, they discovered they were both counselors, were both involved in the same kind of healing, and had the same concerns for humankind, without even saying it. There was something about the look in their eyes that told them of their connection. And there was something that had drawn them together, too. It's one of those many mysteries of life where, through what seems like a chance encounter, exchanges occur that are transformational for both, and lasting bonds are forged.

Linking either role—of provider or seeker—exclusively to one gender or the other does a disservice to all of us. As my friend's story illustrates, women play both roles for each other. Men also play both roles for each other, as my own and many other mentoring experiences illustrate. A woman can be a ship, a man, a safe harbor, and the other way around.

What we appear to be on the outside is only half of what we are on the inside. Within us we have all the qualities and potentialities we need to play

**Exhibit 3.2**
One Story, Two Perspectives, Same Outcome

| Separation | Initiation | Return |
|---|---|---|
| Provider | Provider transformed | Nurturer |
| (prepares) | | (gives back) |
| | (accepts seeker) | |
| | | |
| Seeker | Seeker transformed | Sage |
| (seeks) | (finds provider) | (gives back) |

all the roles possible. Within us we are a whole made up of what is humanly possible. We each gain our individual power and realize our potential from the union of our parts.

Myths of the androgynous gods carry eternal truths about human nature.[12] The Bodhisattva, for example, is made up of the masculine Avalokitesvara and the feminine Kwan Yin. The Zuni god of the pueblo, Awonawilona, is sometimes spoken of as he, but is actually he-she. In Egyptian and Greek myths, the moon deity becomes a goddess but still retains something of her male characteristics. Hermaphrodite, the child of Hermes and Aphrodite, is both female and male. And in the Jewish Kabbalah and the Christian Gnostic gospels, the Word Made Flesh is represented as androgynous.

These androgynous gods-goddesses illustrate, even today, that to move toward wholeness is to become conscious of our own inner seeker and provider, our own ship and safe harbor qualities, to strive to bring them into balance and to express both parts in our lives.

The balance, of knowing both perspectives, of glimpsing wholeness, is achieved on the inner level. Both aspects of our personalities, the provider and the seeker, are what set up and maintain the balance we all desire. They would tell the story of the human journey to wholeness from different perspectives. None of us would be able to achieve our wholeness without both versions.

Recognizing the way of the nest, or safe harbor, in living the pattern allows us to understand the wholeness of the natural process even more. When we tell the one archetypal story from the perspective of the ship, or the seeker, we miss hearing the same story from the safe harbor, or provider, perspective. It can be just as transforming—maybe sometimes even more so—to give, to nurture, than to seek and find. These two versions of the same story are illustrated in Exhibit 3.2.

No matter from what perspective we experience the transformational pattern, we become something other than what we were when we started. The seeker becomes the sage; the provider becomes the nurturer. Each not only has the potential of the other within; each also, as a result of the transformation, has even more to give others. And the same qualities are required of each to complete the transformation: endurance, patience, and submission to the process itself. One blueprint fits all, but since we seem to hear more stories from the perspective of the traveler, we need to hear more versions of the "perspective from the inn" to balance out the ways in which the one story can be experienced and to balance out our understanding of the human experience. Both are equally important.

### LIVING THE PATTERN

Living the pattern of sacred stories requires first of all understanding that there *is* a blueprint to our psychospiritual development and that we are often guided through this pattern whether or not we are aware of it. For the pattern to mean anything and have the impact it is capable of having on us, we must be consciously aware of the pattern when it comes into our lives. This means being aware of experiencing an element of our common human heritage *while* we are experiencing it. It's like being aware of a universal and timeless phenomenon, like the sunrise, while it is happening, or really feeling sadness when that emotion actually comes into our lives. When we experience the present, the moment we are right now living, today's sunrise can become every sunrise, past, present, and future, for us. And when we are consciously aware of an experience of great joy or deep sorrow, that too can become every experience of human joy and sorrow for us.

A universal, often repeated element of human experience, can transform and redirect the course of our lives when we experience it directly and consciously. A core element of mythology, archetypes are still very much alive, even in our world today. When you write your autobiography (in chapter 4), you will find it contains unique events as well as archetypal experiences that you share with other human beings. Understanding the archetypal experiences in your life is the foundation for writing your personal myth.

We all lead universal lives, having experiences that others have had and would recognize as familiar when hearing our story. Any of the problems of life that we can experience today have been around for every generation to experience in their own ways. Problems and difficulties are the heart of archetypal experiences and therefore an essential part of our human experience. Living through any difficult experience in everyday life corresponds to living an archetype of the collective unconscious, because our modern experience reflects the thousands of years of experience our ancestors had before us, struggling and adapting to the circumstances of their existence.

Whether an event that is universal comes to us in a dream, a fantasy, or a vision, it is our conscious experience of such an event that leads to transformation and a change in the way we see the world. The most common archetypes express universally human experiences such as love and hate, birth and death, courtship and separation, change and growth—all transformative in their own way.

We live the pattern of sacred stories by having "real life" experiences and emotions that are archetypal and that bring about a conscious change in our lives and at the same time makes things seem new, or renewed, to us. Such archetypal experiences enter our lives directly and regularly yet on many different levels.[13] We may experience them very subtly on the unconscious level, which means we may have very little or no conscious knowledge of their occurrence in our lives. Or we may experience them on the conscious level, where somehow something about the experience hits us and we know there is something extraordinary about it. This second type of experience has an impact on us, but it may not be a deep, lasting impact. Or we may also experience the archetype on the supraconscious level, where its recognition is sudden, immediate, and deep. This type of experience will likely have a lasting impact on our lives and can be very transformative by itself.

Thus the recognition of an archetypal experience can be subtle, gradual, or immediate. It can even be an awareness that we are participating in the same mystery as our ancestors before us and our descendants after us. The archetypal experience lifts us out of the realm of the occasional and transitory and into the realm of the ultimate and ever-enduring.

## MOMENTS OF TRUTH

Really being in the moment can have a transforming effect on us. Being conscious of a moment when something eternal breaks into our daily existence can transport us out of our temporal life and into the realm of the mythic, where archetypal experiences are found. Such a moment can last forever, because we gain something deep and everlasting from it. This happens often: "The great arch of life whose ultimate aim is the rebirth of the whole personality will consist of many little rebirth moments and rebirth events."[14]

Most of us have had moments so powerful and profound that we tell ourselves, "This is one moment I will never forget for the rest of my life!" It might be a moment of special beauty, a moment of grace, or a significant new accomplishment. It doesn't even have to be that earthshaking; it could be seeing a simple sunrise like we have never seen one before. It is the kind of moment that gives us a feeling of being connected to all life and of becoming aware of something new and eternal within us.

This is the kind of moment that we can recall at any other moment, because its meaning has really penetrated our being. When we deeply experience the archetype, it is always there for us to reflect on and be enriched by over and over again. Our task is to become conscious of such moments before they disappear from our experience.

Living the sacred pattern is experiencing moments in everyday life when something knocks us over the head causing us to see things in a new way. Our status quo gets upset in a way that makes us think about things we never had thought about before. Or, something happens to us that gives us a glimpse of some new possibility in life. These are what Jean Bolen calls "moments of truth."[15] They are moments when we are forced to think about things like why are we here, or what is our purpose.

These moments of truth have the power to set us off on a new direction in life. They indicate that a significant change, even a transformation, is about to happen to us. They can come when we least expect it or when we think we are least prepared to deal with such an opportunity. A moment of truth is what we have when we are about to live the sacred pattern.

Some of our most important moments of truth come when life has given us a terrible blow. We might feel totally abandoned, yet at that moment something unexpected comes along to assist us with what we need to accomplish at that moment. This is a moment that is meant to lead to transformation. It may not look like we are starting out to be a hero or a heroine; we may just be doing the best we can to respond to a disaster. It is *how* we respond, though, that makes all the difference.

Most of the time, when we are in an impossible situation, when our backs are to the wall and there is no visible way of getting out, something or someone comes along at just the right moment to help us out of that situation. In myth, that moment of truth signals the coming of supernatural aid or a guide who will provide exactly what is needed right then. In the religious life, it is called grace. This natural assistance is there for all of us. It is built into the archetypal pattern. We just have to be able to recognize it when it comes.

A moment of truth can be the beginning of individuation, when we begin the process of consciously coming into full awareness of ourselves. Individuation is like being blind and beginning to learn to find your way. The seeing begins with a vague sense of shapes and shadows, then with perceiving things as they are, even in their ugliest nature. Only after this are we able to see things the way we want them to be. Then the more difficult work begins of making things right. That's what often takes a lifetime.

This is what seeing our stories as sacred is all about. As soon as we have become consciously aware of experiencing a major change in our lives or of having found what it is that gives our life its deepest meaning, we begin the process of making our lives sacred and our stories along with it. Being fully engaged in the process of making sacred our stories means being spontaneous, open, in awe of what is and whatever happens and accepting of it, while being able to let any part of it go when its time to go has come.


## A PIECE OF MY STORY

It was in 1970, when I met Joseph Campbell, that I became aware that I was living ageless archetypal themes in my life. When I heard him speak of the mythic journey at Cooper Union, I took it all in, enthralled by what he was illustrating, and suddenly realized that I was at that time living what he was describing.

That wouldn't have been a "moment of truth" for me had it not been for other things that led up to it. In reality, our lives are telling a story before we know enough to ask, "What's the story?"[16] To begin at the beginning, it was a long time before I knew what my story was, or that there were questions to be asked. I am an only child; only many years later did I realize I am like every other child, too. I was too young to remember, but parades of celebration filled the streets the day I was born. The first atomic bomb had turned a world at war into a nuclear village. But peace was elusive, so my life became a subtle quest to find it.

I went through my childhood and adolescence mostly unaware of who I was or what I was doing, even though in Boy Scouts I became an Eagle Scout and got the God and Country award, and in school played sports, had a motorscooter my senior year, graduated, and went to college. It was as if I was sleepwalking through those things.

But there was an earlier clue to my future. When I was about nine, my grandmother stayed with us for awhile and I became fascinated by her commitment to her spiritual life. Her silent, private reading from the *Bible* and *The Upper Room* was a mystery to me. There was something inside my nine-year-old mind, or heart, that wanted to know about something I couldn't grasp. I wanted to know what it was in her experience that had given her such a sense of devotion and commitment to what I came to realize much later was a very special personal spiritual life.

I didn't know it then, but this curiosity set the tone for a major theme in my own life. I know now that what I wanted to know then was what spirituality was, where it came from, how it was developed, and how it is applied in everyday living. I didn't even have those questions in my mind then, but they have become the questions I have been living ever since.

Later, in my second year of college, I discovered I enjoyed philosophy and decided to major in what fascinated me. I not only made the Dean's List, but I began to get a glimpse of how I wanted my story to unfold. I became consciously drawn to people, elders especially, whom I felt had some personal wisdom to share about life. I followed my curiosity to find out how and why people like my grandmother live their lives the way they do. For example, while studying folklore in graduate school I chose to do a life story interview with a traditional farmer and singer from the Catskill Mountains of New York. It is clear to me now that my grandmother influenced my interest in wanting to understand people who had gotten the most out of life.

After I completed my master's degree, I found myself, in the summer of 1969, sailing on the maiden voyage of the Hudson River sloop *Clearwater* from New York to Albany. I was the only non-singing crew member at the time. I had met Pete Seeger the year before, and he had told me about the *Clearwater* project. When the sloop sailed by Long Island he invited me to sail along, agreeing with me that it would be a good idea to document the history of the sloops on the Hudson by interviewing some of the old captains and their families.

That experience reminded me of something else that happened when my grandmother stayed with us. One day I was sitting on my bed daydreaming when I heard a voice say, "Someday you will know God." That voice had remained silent for fifteen years, until my experiences on the *Clearwater*.

This is when my own life turned into a living myth. At twenty-four, my subtle, unconscious quest became a conscious quest and I began asking some new and difficult questions of my life. The *Clearwater* represented my call to adventure, the time in my life when I left behind the familiar and set out on an unknown path, and when I finally began to know and live, and became the author of, my own story. When I was at the tiller sailing the sloop beneath the Rip Van Winkle Bridge, it was as if I had awakened from my own twenty-year slumber. That weekend, in mid-August, the captain of the sloop, a couple of other crew members, and I, took off for Woodstock. But everybody already knows that story.

I lived alone that fall in a cabin in the woods by the river and learned some things from the land around me. On a side trip, when I was with Ramblin' Jack Elliott, a friend from the *Clearwater*, we went to visit Arlo Guthrie at his farm in the Berkshire Mountains. Arlo was as hospitable and gracious a host as you could hope to find anywhere. I returned often and had many wonderful visits with him. On one of those visits, Arlo came downstairs in the morning and said to his wife and me that he had a new song he wanted to sing for us. It was a cloudy, overcast morning and he sang his new song from a piece of paper on the kitchen table. When he sang the line, "Come on, children, all come home/Jesus gonna make you well," the sun came out from behind the clouds and shone right down on the paper. When he finished, he said, "The same thing happened when I wrote the song."

I didn't plan it this way, but during the time right before and after I met Arlo, what was going on in my life seemed pretty amazing to me, and it still does. At the time, it seemed like what mattered most was making sense of my life. That's where most of my energy went. A lot of what I have to say about life stories comes from what I learned from getting at the truth of my own life story. And it is the same for everyone. In your own life story is where you will find *your* truth.

This brings us to the winter of 1969–1970, when my interest in life stories became forever linked with mythology. I discovered a remarkable pattern directing my story. One evening I was walking down 8th Street in New York City, looking in store windows, when a book on mythology caught my eye. I went inside the bookshop and began to page through the book. After awhile, I looked up and a poster caught my eye. It was announcing a lecture by Joseph Campbell, whose book I was reading. The lecture was that evening, and only a few blocks away. I looked at the clock, and found that I had just enough time to walk over there. And that's what I did. It was all spontaneous.

I sat down in the Great Hall at Cooper Union, and as soon as I began to listen to Campbell, it felt as if he were speaking directly to me, as if I were the only one in the room. As he described the mythic journey, everything he said about the similarities between the mythic pattern and certain psychological processes made complete sense because it seemed like my own experiences confirmed everything he was saying. I realized then and there that that was exactly what I was living—the "universal formula" of "separation, initiation, and return."

He described two forms of this pattern. The mythic form is often viewed on its external level: "A hero ventures forth from the world of common day into a region of supernatural wonder: fabulous forces are there encountered and a decisive victory is won: the hero comes back from this mysterious adventure with the power to bestow boons on his fellow men."

The other form, the psychological, takes place primarily on an inner level: first, there is "a break away or departure from the local social order and context; next, a long, deep retreat inward and backward, backward, as it were, in time, and inward, deep into the psyche; a chaotic series of encounters there, darkly terrifying experiences, and presently (if the victim is fortunate) encounters of a centering kind, fulfilling, harmonizing, giving new courage; and then finally, in such fortunate cases, a return journey of rebirth to life."[17]

This is the sacred pattern of myth. When I understood my own experience within this pattern, then my own life, my own story, became sacred, too.

My "departure" to a realm of wonder began that summer with my sail on the *Clearwater*. Fitting in was for me a challenge not only because it involved a break from my familiar surroundings but also because it was like entering a region of supernatural wonder. I had many new "thresholds" to cross.

My "retreat" inward and backward, where I encountered "fabulous forces" and won an inner victory, occurred that fall and winter. I first lived in the cabin in the woods, where I spent many hours in reflection exploring the world of nature around me and facing my own inconsistencies in light of the wholeness I saw around me. Then that winter I lived as a guest in a Franciscan monastery and encountered a spiritual realm entirely new to me that lead ultimately to renewal and helped to make my experience more complete and whole.

While sitting there listening to Joseph Campbell describe the third part of the pattern—that of a "return,"—I had no idea that a few months later I would return to the college I graduated from three years earlier to teach a course on contemporary folk-rock lyrics as poetry to a group of students, some of whom would include a few of my former classmates. With this series of experiences, my own version of the three-part mythic pattern would be complete. And this is what I have since written as my personal myth, *Seasons of the Soul*.

There was no way I could have planned, expected, or anticipated what had happened to me. It was all just there and happened *to* me. I had crossed the threshold into a timeless realm, a realm of universal human experience, and entered the world of transformation. I became conscious of living a major change in my life. What I had to do was see it, really experience it, and then just as joyfully let it go, because my life was going to carry on to the next thing after all that anyway. Seeing the poster in the bookstore announcing Joseph Campbell's talk that evening was for me a moment of truth.

After the talk, I went up and told Campbell how important what he had to say was to me. He responded very warmly and showed a sincere interest in me. We kept in touch for a number of years, and I visited him in his Greenwich Village home a couple of times. His concern and guidance, directly and through his books, had a major impact on my early adult development.

When I saw that poster in the bookstore, there was something that told me that's where I should be at that time, no question about it. I had no idea, though, how much that spontaneous decision to leave the bookstore and attend the talk would influence my life. What it did was to enable a series of serendipitous experiences to continue, which lead me further into a deeper understanding of myself and of my fuller role in the life!

I think of this as a special type of openness, an openness to the mythic life. It's like the princess who followed her ball into the pond where it was retrieved by the frog who later became her prince. When we allow ourselves to be open to a "call," we find ourselves living out mythic themes and patterns: That's the truth I have found in my life, and that's why personal mythmaking seems like such an important part of life storytelling to me. That's where chapters 5 and 6 of this book come in: they describe how we can recognize some of those universal themes that may have already played themselves out in our lives.

In 1974, after teaching that course on folk-rock lyrics as poetry, I edited an anthology of some of those song lyrics and arranged them according to the mythological journey of the hero (*Songs of the Open Road*). In taking a close look at the lyrics, I found that the songwriters were expressing their personal myths—their archetypal experiences that mirrored part or all of the pattern Campbell described as the monomyth. There was another set of real people living mythic lives.

A little while later, I began giving workshops and courses on personal mythmaking to groups of adults of all ages in places like the University of New Hampshire, the University of Chicago, and now the University of Southern Maine (USM). They confirmed for me that the archetypal pattern I had experienced in my life is indeed a living human pattern that is shared by many, either consciously or unconsciously, as we live our lives in this complicated modern world.

At USM, I wanted to have a framework within which students could experience some of the joy, wonder and power of really getting to know themselves and others as storymakers, as I had.

This is how the Center for the Study of Lives came into being in January of 1988, to record, preserve, and pass on the life stories of people of all ages and backgrounds. Through the life story interviews my students have done, we now have an archive of over 200 life stories in the Center. What I do now is a very strong thread in my own life story.

I feel extremely fortunate to be in the position of helping to give others the gift of stories. I have had many remarkable women and men in my classes over the years, people mostly in their thirties and forties, a few in their sixties and seventies. All express ways in which they have continued to grow as adults. A student recently said in class, while we were discussing the autobiographical exercise they had just brought in, "I got more out of this than I did in six months of counseling." Another student said, "I wanted everything else to stop while I was writing this paper."

Over the past twenty-five years or so, I have read hundreds of life stories. I have come to know well their power. Every time I hear or read one, I am awestruck and feel like I have been given a precious gift. I am convinced that today's life stories are as spellbinding, as marvelous, and as wonderful as any classic myth or folktale ever was.

## MAKING OUR STORIES SACRED

What the archetype, or the sacred pattern, ultimately is or does for us depends on our attitude toward it, how we experience it. We can either experience the archetype as light or dark, good or bad, or as growth promoting or growth inhibiting. What we do with it depends on our attitude or our emotional state.

The sacred pattern really makes its connection with us through our emotions.[18] My mental and emotional conditions at the moment an archetype appears in my life determines the effect it has on me. If I am in a negative state of being, the archetypal experience could inhibit what it is meant to achieve for me; if I am not conscious of its presence at all, it will likely have no effect on my life; if however, I am open to the experience for its own sake and at least recognize a bit of its wonder, it can become transformative and achieve what it was given to me for.

The message the sacred pattern brings to us is the message of protection, of guidance, and of salvation.[19] That pattern entering our lives signals release from a confining situation; it signals an opening into an expanded region, an expanded consciousness, or the possibility of another step in our evolutionary path. It represents the opportunity for a new status in life.

We live the pattern of the archetype when we consciously experience a transition in our lives that takes us from one state of being to another. This is what makes our lives universal, mythic, and connected to all others. This is also the essence of the process of individuation. We are led to some deep personal truths that guide our daily lives and give us a clear sense of purpose and meaning in life. We find a comfortable focus to our lives and an accompanying stability. There is little that can shake us from our convictions.

We make our stories sacred by identifying the events and experiences in our lives that have made us into someone different than who we were. Finding metaphors that help us see the meaning in our lives and that give our life story a shape that connects it to other enduring stories helps to make our story sacred. Becoming intimately familiar with the pattern that brings about transformation, looking for and recognizing those moments of truth when we find ourselves at a crossroads in our lives, is what making our stories sacred is all about.

Making our stories sacred involves an interior odyssey where we learn to embrace our own inner demons. It is a process leading to a rebirth where the "spirit" is no longer neglected. This process proceeds slowly, step by step, affecting us first in one part and then in another until gradually we might begin to feel the whole affected.

Making our stories sacred means consciously acknowledging the experience of a personal struggle, ordeal, or quest, where little by little we broaden our scope of consciousness, experience a symbolic "death," attain a greater inner freedom, and then enter into the grace of "rebirth." This is a process that every human being can know firsthand, every time we leave behind an old status, an old image of ourselves, or an old world view, and take on a new view of ourselves or the world.

This understanding not only gives us a clearer view of our own life, it also helps to make our own life experience feel more special, important, and even sacred, too. When we can clearly identify the movement from order to disorder and back to order in our lives and the resolution of our own conflicts, we have found the universal in the unique and the sacred in the personal. When this happens, we have felt the transformative power of stories, and we become consciously aware of the sacred operating in our lives. (This is a process we will carry out in full in chapters 6 and 7.)

Stories fulfill their original and highest purpose when they express the sacred, the timeless, within us. What we all yearn for most is to hear the voice of our own soul, to understand what has moved us the most deeply. We also yearn to hear this same voice in others, for the same reasons. We want to be able to tell others and hear from others what it is that has made us who we are at our essence.

We want to be able to share with others what it is, what single experience it is, that has given us our greatest joy. Though this is where words seem to fail us, we are often surprised by the insights the effort brings us. When we are aware of hearing the voice of our soul speaking through a story, we feel as never before a connection, a confirmation that we are part of one great interconnected creation.

Getting to our sacred story, to the story of our soul, no matter how much struggle or frustration it involves, always awakens noble sentiments within us and spurs us on toward carrying out what we see as our highest purpose. Sharing our sacred story is much more than individual expression; it is an expression of our humanness, of what we have in common with others. It becomes a validation that we are all related.

To search through our experience fully and deeply enough so that we arrive at a sense of peace when we complete the quest; to get to the core of our life, to feel our inner harmony, to recognize and acknowledge our link with what has given us life and with others sharing our wider home with us; this is soul-making. Telling this story is sacred storytelling. Acting upon this new knowledge of ourselves, and carrying it out the rest of our lives in everything we do, is living in a sacred manner.

## NOTES

1. Jacobi, *The psychology of C. G. Jung*, p. 105.
2. Waddington, *The strategy of the genes*.
3. Campbell, *Myths to live by*, p. 211.
4. van Gennep, *The rites of passage*.
5. Eliade, *Rites and symbols of initiation*.
6. Campbell, *The hero with a thousand faces*, p. 30.
7. Underhill, *Mysticism*.
8. Jacobi, *The way of individuation*.
9. Bridges, *Transitions*.
10. Morrison, Interview, with Claudia Tate.
11. Sarton, *A world of light*.
12. Campbell, *The hero with a thousand faces*, pp. 151–53.

13. Jacobi, *Complex archetype symbol*, pp. 127–28.

14. Jacobi, *The way of individuation*, p. 61.

15. Jean Bolen spoke of "moments of truth" in a talk given in Portland, Maine, April 12, 1991, "The hero and heroine in everyperson: The mythic dimensions of ordinary life," sponsored by the C.G. Jung Center, Brunswick, Maine.

16. Keen, *Fire in the belly*, p. 130; also from a talk entitled "Hymn to an unknown god," Psyche and Soul Conference, The Findhorn Foundation, Inverness, Scotland (March 1989).

17. The talk by Joseph Campbell is published as chapter 10 in *Myths to live by*.

18. Jung, *Psychological reflections*, p. 43.

19. Jacobi, *The way of individuation*, pp .15–20, 78–81; and *The psychology of C. G. Jung*, pp. 48–49, 107.

**II**

# THE GIFT OF STORIES

Their story, yours, mine—it's what we all carry with us on this trip we take, and we owe it to each other to respect our stories and learn from them.

—William Carlos Williams

# 4

## *Giving Yourself Your Own Story: Writing Autobiographically*

> I can shake off everything if I write; my sorrows disappear, my courage
> is reborn. But will I ever be able to write anything great?[1]

When we write autobiographically—when we explore our own inner realms, dig deep into ourselves, and bring out what lies buried in our hearts—we write about the experiences and feelings that are most important to us. Writing about ourselves in this way involves us in a process of "soul-making," because we evoke the emotions and experiences—of crisis and opportunity, of love and dying, of values and truth—that give life a deeper meaning.[2] Writing about these things is a spiritual endeavor, because it gets us in touch with our ultimate concerns and helps us realize that we are more than we thought. And when this happens, does it really matter if we write anything great?

All autobiographical writing is spiritual. By the time we are old enough, mature enough, or desirous enough to think reflectively about our own experience, put it in order, and give voice to it, everything that has happened to us comes into play as part of the ongoing endeavor to discover, or uncover, who we are at our core. And when we tell the truth about ourselves, we come to a clearer understanding of who we really are. In this way we become more courageous, more authentic, and more alive. We become more of who we already are. Automatically, through this process, we get more in touch with our own spirituality.

When we hear each other's truth, we both gain something very important. When we become more conscious of ourselves, and of others, we come to understand more about the experience of all human beings. Expressing our personal truth is what we each owe ourselves, perhaps more than anything else.

Our stories are always within us waiting to come out and enrich our own lives and the lives of others. They emerge, evolve, and change right along with us as we grow and mature. We become the author of our own life story when we begin to take conscious control of our life and bring our story out and actually share it with others. At six, we are less the author of our story than we are at twenty-six or sixty-six because at six we probably have less to do with the circumstances of our life then than we do after we've been out on our own.

When we tell the story of our birth, family, cultural influences, and childhood, we may not be telling our story in terms of what we did but rather the story of what happened to us then, since we were pretty much dependent upon the circumstances we were born into. Our lives at this point are primarily determined for us. We have very little authorship, or control, over our lives during childhood. Our particular circumstances act more upon us than we do upon them, as children.

Early in childhood, however, we acquire an "autobiographical memory."[3] At about age three or four, we begin to relate our own experiences to others and to file these events in our store of memories. We learn in the normal course of events what a story is and that it consists of both structure and scripts that are repeated over and over. Eventually, we begin to cast our own experience, our autobiographical memory, within this structure.

It may only be by adolescence, when we start figuring out who we really are, by what identity we would like to be known, and what we want to do with our lives, that we begin to take an active role in becoming the author of our own life story. With adolescence and the identity formation process, we become aware that our life is taking a shape that is more ours. We are able to look ahead as well as backward in our lives, and integrate past, present, and future into the story of our life. We can look ahead with a bit more realism and anticipate, if not plan out, how we would like the rest of our story to unfold. We begin to understand that our story is always in process, as are we, of expanding and changing.

From that point on, through young adulthood, we become familiar with the role that change and transition plays in our lives. We have a clearer sense, by then, of what is and is not within our control and therefore of what are some of the key events and incidents in our life story. We become more concerned with our past and want to be sure that all parts of our life fit together to match the way we see ourselves.

By middle age, with half our life behind us, we get a sense of what we have or have not yet accomplished and how this fits in with the story line we might have anticipated twenty years earlier when we first began to think about how we wanted our life to unfold. There may be a sense of accomplishment and satisfaction with how closely our life story is unfolding compared to what we had envisioned. Or there may suddenly arise a sense of urgency around the lack of time left and the formidable challenge before us to finally seize control of our life before it's really too late, maybe make dramatic changes and salvage the story we feel we deserve or are capable of living to tell about later. Or, if we are really lucky, we may get to the mid-point of our life and discover that the way the story is turning out is even better than what we had imagined. In whichever case, we acknowledge that we are clearly the author of our life story now, and that our story does sound somewhat familiar to us and to others who hear it because it is told within a framework with which we are all familiar.

By our seventies and eighties, with fewer years ahead of us and more behind us, our task is to finally accept and acknowledge not only that there is clearly a beginning, a middle, and an end to our story, but that it seems to have had just as clear a plot. The drama of the story may be nearly complete, but this is when we may want to put the finishing touch, like an epilogue, on our story.

Being able to see our life as a whole helps us accept not only the life we have lived but also the role we have had as author of the entire story, even the early years when we were not in control of our life. If we can be happy with and accept the job we did as author of our story, and perhaps write the closing paragraph to it that would make it a story we can live *and* die with, that would give our life the integrity and fulfillment it deserves.

There are many ways we can tell our story to get at the meaning in our lives, to integrate the pieces of our lives, and to connect our experience to that of others. It is important for us to find our own style, our own particular way of expressing our story that feels right and natural to us. St. Augustine used the confessional. Dante used allegory. Thoreau wrote about himself in the context of nature. Today many seem comfortable presenting their memories, their story, as autobiographical fiction, impressionistically presenting the self in the way they want others to know them.

Yet, this is what we have always done. We can only present what we want of ourselves in the way we want to. Most life storytelling is a combination of all of these ways, thereby blurring the boundaries between autobiography, memoir, journal writing, and other forms of writing about the self.

Sometimes there can even be a blur between a serious and a lighthearted approach to life storytelling. The lighthearted can turn out to have its serious side and the serious its irony, if not lightness. Wisdom, insight, and depth can be clothed in any garment. The similarity in intent between two very different styles can be quite striking.

Take for example the writing of Etty Hillesum, a Jewish woman in her late twenties who died at Auschwitz. Her diaries of 1941–43 present a self deeply sensitive to everything that touches her life. Paradoxically, the total destruction that was going on all around her was not her focus. She put all of her writing within the context of her expanding spiritual awareness, which led her to the source of her existence:

> Life is composed of tales waiting to be retold by me. Oh, what nonsense—I don't really know anything. . . . A hard life is in store for me. Sometimes I don't feel like carrying on. At the moments when I feel I know exactly what is going to happen to me, what life will be like, I get so tired and feel no need to experience things as they come. But life always gains the upper hand, and then I find everything "interesting" and exciting again and I am full of courage and full of ideas. . . .
>
> Life and human relationships are full of subtleties. I know that there is nothing absolute or objectively valid, that knowledge must seep into your blood, into your self, not just into your head, that you must live it. And here I always come back to what one should strive after with all one's might: one must marry one's feelings to one's beliefs and ideas. That is probably the only way to achieve a measure of harmony in one's life. . . .
>
> Why shouldn't one feel an immense, tender ecstasy of love for the spring, or for all humanity? And one can befriend the winter, too, or a town, or a country. . . . "After this war, two torrents will be unleashed on the world: a torrent of loving-kindness and a torrent of hatred." And then I knew: I should take the field against hatred. I would love to be like the lilies of the field. Someone who managed to read this age correctly would surely have learned just this: to be like a lily of the field.[4]

Etty Hillesum, though surrounded by so much human misery and barbed wire, was a woman with a spirit that grew lighter and brighter in that environment. "The signs of the times . . . did not seem meaningless to" her, and her writings helped her make sense of her immediate inner world.

Contrast this to the times and style of Arlo Guthrie. He is a master of fancifulness, whose stories seem to be aimed at our funny bone. He has been writing his own autobiographical songs since he was a teenager. A few years ago, he created a newsletter for his fans and called it the *Rolling Blunder Review*. In it are some humorously profound pieces of reflective writing. Here's an example:

### My Oughtabiography
### by Arlo Guthrie

I was born with a guitar in one hand in Coney Island, which is in the good part of Brooklyn, New York. It was during the summer of 1947. My parents (Woody Guthrie & Marjorie Mazia Greenblatt) were both very creative people and outstanding in their respective fields, which explains my life. My father notes that I screamed a lot and that I also banged on things. It became my mission in life.

I made some money when I was younger (in my early twenties) screaming and banging on things and spent most of it to purchase an old farm in Massachusetts, so that I could have a field to stand out in also. I got married, helped raise four strange kids, and wrote lots of songs on my farm. I continue my mission even today.

People want to know the stupidest things about me sometimes. I even overheard someone recently say of me, "I thought he bought the farm." I can't imagine why they're saying that NOW! I bought it 20 years ago. It's just not all paid off yet. This explains why I still travel around a lot and why I'm working most of the time.

In my free time I play business with my friends. In 1986 we began Rising Son Records. I also began writing a lot, and publish a quarterly magazine to get all the stuff off my desk.

My personal life is somewhat of a mystery, even to me. Although it's fun to be mysterious at times, it isn't always convenient. People always want to know what you are, as if it made some kind of difference. Lots of people want to have something special in common with folksingers. They'd like to share their views on religion, pollution, nuclear power, human rights, truth, justice, and the American way with someone who sees things the same way.

I have come to the conclusion that we are all one person with a few billion faces so we can see things in lots of different ways. I guess there really isn't any mystery to me at all, unless I think of myself as being all alone.

When I allow myself to believe I'm by myself (next to me), I write things to myself. Then I read this stuff and wonder.[5]

If we really understand what each is saying, there is a striking similarity of intent, if not style, in the message both Etty Hillesum and Arlo Guthrie wish to convey in their autobiographical writing. Arlo Guthrie is a self-made mystic and a natural-born humorist. They make for a wonderful blending of qualities. How he expresses himself is a delight to experience, whether it is in person or on paper.

The range of styles that we can draw on to tell our own story is vast. The best we can do is try to combine our own natural style and qualities with those experiences and qualities we acquire along the way to tell our story in the way that is most like us.

Writing autobiographically can come to us as a gift. That's the way it came to me. I found myself doing it one day without really thinking about it. I didn't know what I was going to say, but I discovered that I was writing about the really important things in my life at that time.

Annie Dillard says, "At its best, the sensation of writing is that of any unmerited grace. It is handed to you, but only if you look for it. You search, you break your heart, your back, your brain, and then—and only then—is it handed to you."[6]

I had been a writer before. I wrote sports stories for my school newspaper. But I carried on with my life, looking for something more. The events I was living when I found myself writing autobiographically forced me to answer the questions that I hadn't even asked yet.

This was the period in my life I later wrote as my personal myth. It was 1969, and I was living as a guest in a Franciscan monastery. I had been given a cell of my own with the friars when I was in between places while doing research for the Hudson River Sloop Restoration. Everything I experienced in the monastery was new to me, and that's where I began my autobiographical writing.

One morning, I woke up, sat up, put my feet on the floor, thought for a moment, grabbed my pencil and paper, and wrote my first poem. What I wrote about were my inner experiences of the moment, living in the monastery. Everything around me, like the meaning of the crucifix and the habits the friars wore, were questions wanting to be answered. So I reflected and wrote about what was going on in the moment. That created a direct link with my spiritual self.

I found out, as Natalie Goldberg had, that "what's in front of you is a good beginning."[7] I came upon my own autobiographical writing rather serendipitously. It is not the same for everyone. Some people plan it out for a long time. I didn't sit down and look at the blank paper forever. It just happened when I was ready for it to happen. And then it flowed.

My thoughts and writing went naturally and automatically to that place where I could try to answer the important questions for me. I see autobiographical writing as a process that begins on the inside. We have to be aware of this and aid the process in whatever way we can. But this may be somehow different for each of us.

I have experienced much struggle as well as reward in my autobiographical writing. The struggle occurs because we have a vision of what is possible. The reward comes when we follow some kind of structure to help us accomplish what we envision. The following suggestions may help you achieve what you want. The autobiographical exercises in the second part of this chapter are the ones I use in most of my classes. They are designed to bring out many of the things that lie buried in your heart.

My students seem to learn something more about themselves each time they write autobiographically of their pain, their struggles, and their triumphs. I value what they have to say about themselves, and I learn a great deal about how we grow and adapt each time I read anyone's autobiographical reflections. I consider it an honor to be able to encourage and support others in writing about their lives from their heart and to read their wonderful, inspiring, and powerful thoughts.


## SUGGESTIONS FOR GETTING STARTED

I haven't called these ground rules for writing, because being grounded is not necessarily the best thing when writing autobiographically. Nor is having rules; they imply restrictions. Maybe the only rule we need for writing about ourselves is: Don't make any rules. The image of feeling free enough to move around a bit more than you could on the ground, of feeling as though you can look down on yourself from above and get a new perspective on yourself is more of what we are after, I think. What you really need in writing about yourself, along with this sense of freedom, is a feeling of being inspired. That's what enthusiasm is all about—being filled with spirit and wanting to express yourself with a spirit of wonder, joy, and acceptance. Another side of inspiration is motivation: we are most motivated by whatever it is that most inspires us. We need to look for those aspects of our lives that most fill us with the desire or need to share them with others. These suggestions are meant to fuel your inspiration and motivation so you will be on the road to writing deeply and truthfully about yourself.

### Write for Yourself, First

Writing your life story is for your own satisfaction, your own enjoyment. You are not trying to impress or please anyone but yourself. Your story is for you, primarily; chances are it will also be for your family, friends, or even your community. But if you aren't happy with it, maybe the others won't be, either. When others are enriched by your story, that's the icing on the cake. But since you are the one you are writing for, do it the way that makes you feel good. You write for and about your self to maintain a balance in your life. When you pull up what is within you, you offset the impersonal all around you. Author Christina Baldwin began her journal writing at age twelve in a secret annex of the basement in her home after seeing a production of *The Diary of Anne Frank* that had left her "awash with grief."[8]

### Listen for Your Inner Voice

What you really want to be able to do is express yourself authentically and distinctly, in a manner that is unique to you, with a "voice" that is your own.[9] When you free yourself from the limiting, restrictive injunctions you might have been taught about writing, when you let your natural urge for self-expression go and express your deepest, most meaningful experience many times over, year after year, you may find your own unique, inner voice. It is not an easy find, but it is your link with what is personally sacred within you. It is your voice that resonates with your rhythm, your cadence, your style, and your truth.

The path to your inner voice begins with creating around and within you a contemplative silence. When you seek silence and nothing else and are silent with your self long enough, thinking one thought at a time—or better yet, no thoughts at all—you will come to a place of calm where you will hear your inner voice, and it will guide you and give you words of truth and insight. From this place of inner solitude you will bring forth your inner wisdom and discover who and what you really are.

When the quest for your inner voice begins in silence, you can put down on your paper the first thoughts that come into your mind from that place of deep solitude. You could let the first few minutes be a kind of "freewriting," where you record whatever comes out of your silence first. The important thing is to get something down so that what is happening for you becomes clear. At some later point, you will be able to say, "yes, this *is* me!".

Sometimes, this voice may even be quite loud, but it is often we who are deaf to it. Our inner voice may actually be our intuition calling out to us from our place of inner certainty. Without showing us any facts or giving us any reason at all, our inner voice, our intuition, may be speaking to us of an inner truth that we need to know or be aware of, even in the case of long-forgotten memories of our past.

It is difficult sometimes to separate intuition from idle imaginations. But what we are looking for as our inner voice, our direct perception of an inner truth, comes to us most often in our moments of calm, is supportive rather than judgmental, and in some way challenges us, yet gives us a sense of having already known what it is revealing to us. Our inner voice comes from a sacred place within but can only succeed to work with and for us if we hear it and follow it. "Out of my most inward and most deeply feeling self" is where Eudora Welty found her "voice."[10]

### Let Your Deepest Feelings Be Your Guide

Our real, inner, deep feelings are our own best teachers about who we really are. We may most often find these in our memories of childhood. It is there that many of our most deeply felt, core experiences lie. These and other memories of our most meaningful moments since childhood will be the fuel for the most powerful, moving writing we will ever do. Writing about these core memories takes us right back to those feelings we had then as well as how we are feeling about them now.

If the memories come but the feelings don't, you may have to reconstruct the experience in your mind and ask yourself some difficult questions, like: What was I really feeling when that happened? What circumstances caused me to feel this way? Why would those circumstances make me feel this way? Am I still feeling that way now about what happened then? If you really reflect on these questions, you will probably come up with something new. The wider the range of our emotions about something, the more complete our thought and expression will be about it, too. One method for evoking feelings is *clustering*, or starting with one key term and adding to that other words that the key term reminds you of. Clustering generates fresh perceptions, meaningful patterns, a childlike wondering and innocence, choices, and an unimpeded flow of images, ideas, and memories that are all emotionally tinged.

## Recall and Explore Your Memories

Putting our memories down on paper gives us insight into the person we are. Having a sense of where we've come from and what has been most important to us gives us a center, a focus, and a clearer direction. All kinds of memories are important. Pleasant memories are a source of joy and strength; writing about these can build upon and add to that joy and sustain us in difficult times. Unpleasant memories can also be sources of strength; when we write about these, we transform them into something known, manageable, and controllable. They no longer control us or restrict us in some way. Making sense now of why they were once unpleasant for us gives us a new reason to feel better about ourselves.

Reflecting upon and then writing about our memories is a way to explore them that makes them clearer and more understandable and more acceptable to us. Through exploring our memories on paper, we often come to a resolution about them that we might not have had before. We give them a shape that fits our present perception of things, which is probably very different than was our perception when that memory occurred.

One way to explore memories is first to create a memory bank. You can start with a list of themes or general topics, like first-time events, people, scenes, trips, triumphs, struggles, and revelations. Then fill out each one with as many brief memories as you can remember under that topic, listing only a phrase or sentence at first. From the list of actual brief memories you generate under each topic, you can then explore any of them by writing about them in detail when you are ready.

## Get to the Heart of the Matter

When we explore our memories, our goal could be, as it was for Anne Frank, to get at what lies buried in our heart. After all, it's not the writing that really matters. It's life, the lived experience, that inspires and drives us to write what is most important. We have to remember that we would not have anything to write about if we hadn't had something significant to live in the first place.

Another goal could be looking first for those experiences that make up our personally sacred moments. These are the ones resting in our heart that make up the real heart of our experience. These are the times in our life when we have felt watched over, protected, guided, connected, rewarded, generous, and giving. They are also moments of new beginnings, of troubled difficult times, of times when we were in control of everything in our lives, and even times when things were out of control for us. They are sacred moments because they are what make up our core experience, they are the moments that have made us more whole, more of who we really are.

The details and feelings of these moments need to be shared with others because they are what is most important to us and what will last the longest in our lives. To get at the feelings of what really matters for us, we may have to ask ourselves some probing questions, like: What is it about my life that will be as important ten, twenty, or thirty years from now as it seems to be right now? Who has been with me in my sacred moments? What role have these moments played in my life? What has made me feel the most connected to life? What is the greatest gift I have been given? What is the gift I have given others? When have I been most in control of my life? When have I been most out of control in my life?

At the heart of life is conflict, change, and growth. If we put the emphasis on the interaction between the people involved in our story at these times, on what was really going on between them, on the relationships and what they were really like, we get at what really mattered to us. Or, if we focus on the interaction within us, between the parts of our selves that might have been torn over some issue or decision, then we find the heart of our life. Our feelings from this place tell a story that is heartfelt, one that speaks most directly to others.


### Write the Way You Talk

Most of us speak more than we write. We are accustomed to the way we talk. We have done that all our lives. Things flow a lot easier for us that way. When we write autobiographically, all we have to do is be clear and be ourselves. We don't have to worry about how what we write sounds. Style is not as important as communication of truth. Don't lose a lot of time thinking and rethinking a thought you might put down on paper, just put it down. There is plenty of time later to go back and revise it if you need to. All you have to think about is being sure that your story sounds like you. Let your speaking voice become your writing voice.


### Be Creative, Imaginative, and Even Fanciful

Don't feel trapped by form, style, genre, or even the facts. Most of our memories seem to come back to us in a creative, imaginative form, anyway, so it would be natural to want to write creatively, imaginatively, and maybe even fancifully at times. Autobiographical writing can be fun as well as informative. You might want to try different forms of writing about yourself, such as allegorical, impressionistic, or maybe fairy-tale style. Autobiographical poetry can be just as effective as prose, or the other way around. Style in autobiography is not as important as letting your writing flow and being yourself.

In our imagination, we can reconstruct how we think we might have felt during a particularly important but vague memory. How we imagine we felt or remembered something can be just as important or valid as what actually did happen. We may never be able to determine the difference, anyway. If you imagine something that could have happened, but didn't, and write about it, that could also be very revealing and maybe even liberating. Letting your imagination take you where it wants to go could have the same effect on your life now as writing about something that really happened. For example, it could help you feel better now to write about an event in your childhood where you finally did rebel, take charge, or stand your ground against oppressors, even though you may not have actually had that experience. If you never imagine, you may never discover the feelings connected with your imaginings.

If it is difficult for you to be creative or fanciful, then just be you. But don't be tight. As Brenda Ueland has suggested, "Be careless, reckless! Be a lion, be a pirate! Write any old way."[11] In other words, don't be scared, don't be self-conscious, don't be shy. If you have been taught composition, plot, and structure, forget it. Just let your own order and unity emerge.

### Try Humor Once in a While

Sometimes life is too serious to take it seriously all the time. But can't irony, parody, or humor be serious, too? What about humor that allows us to see even the serious from a different angle? It lifts the serious out of a serious situation to let us see it from a lighter perspective. It shows us a new and probably important perspective that we might not have been able to see from our usual angle of seriousness. To some writers, humor is the essential work; it is a special way of saying the joke is no joke. Humor can help us see a hidden truth about life. And once we've really seen a truth through the guise of humor, we are very likely never to forget it.[12]

Our life stories, too, can reflect a balance of the serious and the light-hearted. But only a small dose of humor is needed to create this balance. Don't use it too much, or it will lose its appeal and power fast. Besides, it is not easy for most of us to find a funny way to say some things. But then again, anything some of us say comes out sounding funny, too.

One of the ways we can find and express the humor in our lives is to exaggerate what actually happened to give greater emphasis to a point we want to make. Something like, "We didn't have a house the size of Rhode Island, but it wasn't the poorhouse, either."

A general guideline, though, is use humor only in relation to the simple, common, everyday things that everybody does. That way, things like eating, sleeping, raising a family, and making money, can be made amusing by focusing on the gap between what we might expect and what actually happens sometimes, because anyone will be able to relate to that. Find the irony or the humorous in what you know to be true, and that will connect with more people than trying to find the outlandish and using that. Simple surprise is the secret to successful humor. Strive for your own truth, and maybe a little humor will ease its way naturally into your story. It's not worth struggling over. Besides, humor is only in the ear of the listener.

### Look for Connections in Your Life

We really write about ourselves to understand who we are. We do this by understanding how our past, present, and future all fit together as a whole and how this makes up the story of our life. When we discover how everything merges and meshes in our lives, we solve the mystery of making the random purposeful. When we can make the chaotic clear and make connections where there were none before, we empower ourselves.

Connections are found where there is the most meaning in our lives. The greatest meaning is usually found at times of shifts, changes, or transitions. When one thing ends and another begins, it may seem like there is discontinuity in our life, but when we really look at those times we see that the shift actually recreates the connection that was already there. A connection between adolescence and adulthood, for example, might be college. That is what gives greater meaning to both and may make the random events of our adolescence appear more clear after we have found our place in adulthood.

Connections in our lives are like threads in a weaving. Some threads stand out because they are different colors, some stand out because of the way they recur over and over. But they are not always visible. Some threads make a strong statement in the weaving, then disappear for awhile. Even though they are not on the surface all the time, they remain a vital part of the pattern and reemerge at various times. The pattern consists of the meaningful repetition of a theme.

That's the way it is in looking for connections in our life. We look for what stands out from everything else, what recurs most often, and what can be followed for the longest period of time in our lives. We look for a pattern in our lives. We look for themes, and we look for the unifying threads that pull the past, present, and future together as one ongoing moment. The themes, or issues, that recur throughout our lives are the strong threads that make the connections recognizable.

In looking back to your childhood, you may recall an event, an issue, or a theme that has appeared more than once, maybe even often, in your life and is still present. For example, a nurse began her personal myth by writing, "As far back as I can remember, I have always felt inwardly guided that my sole purpose in life is to love others and assist others in any way I can. I was blessed with a loving, supportive family and a relatively happy childhood." This theme, of feeling guided and of having a sole purpose in life, is the unifying thread that connects her life as a whole and puts everything in perspective.

*Reread this list of suggestions often until writing autobiographically becomes natural.* With practice, you may get to the point of doing what works for you without thinking too much about it. Then, your autobiographical writing will flow, and your writing may become part of the flow of your life.

## WRITING A LIFE

The exercises and samples of autobiographical writing that follow are designed to help you find a way of writing about yourself that is comfortable for you. They serve two general functions: to help you get more in touch with the truth of your life, as you see it; and to help you view your life as a whole so as to see better the beginning, muddle, and resolution of your life story.

Overall, the exercises are meant to get at who you are at your essence, to help you discover what is personally sacred, what your spirit wants to speak to you of. These exercises should help you focus on your spiritual, or inner life. If effective, they will help you get at who you are at your center, at your core.

Out of this may come a greater understanding of your life theme and major issues. The strong threads will appear more evident, enabling you to focus on those more important issues that provide your life's deepest continuity for you. Being able to identify those threads of continuity in your life, as well as any possible breaks with that continuity or places of discontinuity, will deepen even more your understanding of your life as a whole.[13]

The exercises offered here are not meant to add up to a complete life story. They may come close, but it will be in pieces. You could easily weave the key pieces you come up with from these exercises into a flowing, connected narrative that makes up the core of your entire life story.

One of your objectives could be to find your story, another to name your story. While you are in the process of recalling and writing your story, keep in mind these questions: What is the essence of your story? What is the one thing it says most clearly about you? What themes are most central to your experience? How do you see yourself through all of what you write? And finally, what do you want to do with what your story tells you about you?

## LOOKING AT YOUR LIFE AS A WHOLE

A good way to begin is with a sense of where you have come from, where you want to be heading, and what your goals are for the process you are embarking upon. Think of this as the start of a journey. If you know where you want to go, you have a better chance of getting there. The way to plan out the journey that lies ahead is to first ask yourself some key questions, then step back and look over your life as a whole, from afar. A bird's-eye view of your life often gives a much more insightful perspective with which to begin the process.

What follows are some preliminary questions to think about and to help guide your autobiographical writing. Then there are three different approaches to get a sense of where you have come from before looking at selected parts of it up close in the next section. One approach is imaginative, one is artful, and one is linear. Choose the one that seems to work best for you in getting your story started.

### First Thoughts

A few moments of focused reflection in the beginning can help to uncover themes and threads that give your life meaning. Find a quiet place where you can spend some time with these questions.

What is at the heart of your feelings, right now?

What is it about life stories and personal mythmaking that interests you the most? What part of your life experience do you most want to explore further? What would you like to get out of this experience, and what do you have to give to it?

Be aware of your inner thoughts and the feelings connected to them. After these have settled, write down your insights and the goals you have come up with for yourself for this process.

### Once Upon a Time . . .

Think of your entire life experience in terms of what stands out about you the most or what characterizes you the best. Then tell this in the form of a fairy tale, or mythic story, beginning with, "Once upon a time. . . . " Try to make it as concise as you can, a story of three sentences, three paragraphs, or three pages, that captures the real, inner you or some important aspect of your life. It could be a glimpse of the highlights of your life, a life theme, or a particularly important time in your life.

### The Tree of Life

Draw a tree that represents the roots, trunk, branches, leaves, and blossoms of your life. Identify and label all the parts of the tree, including branches taken and branches not taken, and maybe some yet to be taken. When you have completed drawing and labeling your tree, then write a brief story about all the parts of your tree that you have drawn. You might include the formative experience of your life as part of your trunk, the major branching points in your life, as well as the fruits, blossoms, gifts, and accomplishments of your life.

## Chapters of Your Life

This is a variation on drawing a timeline of your life. It goes into more depth than just listing the important events of your life, year by year. Let's begin with the idea of your life as a book, consisting of a certain number of chapters. Each chapter may take up a different amount of time in your life. Using the timeline, first think of those years in your life that hang together in whatever way as separate and distinct periods, each characterized by something special. Then divide your life into those distinguishable periods, or chapters, by drawing vertical lines from the top to the bottom to separate each chapter, with the years for each chapter on the birth to present line. You will end up with a series of vertical columns, each labeled by a grouping of years in your life that just seem to go together. To get at more of what happened during each chapter, list the most significant events and people during each period. (What was important about these events and people?) Then, briefly describe the issue or theme that was most important during each period. Then, briefly describe the feeling that was dominant during each period. (In general, about yourself, and about others around you.) Then, describe what you wanted most during each period and what you actually achieved. Finally, give each chapter a title. (See Exhibit 4.1.)

## LOOKING BACK

Life can only be understood backwards, but it must be lived forward.[14]

Reflection upon past experience gives us a deeper understanding of what that experience has meant for us over a lifetime. The more we reflect on events in our life, and the longer the period of time we do this, the clearer they become and the more appreciation we have of them. This is one of the ways we gain greater meaning in life. The closer we get to what actually happened in our life, the more convincing and exciting our writing about it will be.

Drawing from the fertile material of childhood, youth, and adulthood that has led us through the many changes, passages, and transitions of those years will yield rich autobiographical writing. The most resonant memories are of those experiences or events that have caused us to expand and deepen our understanding of ourselves and our sense of purpose or meaning in life.

By directing your thoughts first toward these, you will become a writer or storyteller who is not only intriguing but also someone who others would think of as worth getting to know. As you try out the following exercises, open the floodgates to your memory bank, really see the images and pictures from your childhood and adolescence and maybe even the

**Exhibit 4.1**
**Chapters of Your Life**

| BIRTH | PRESENT |
| --- | --- |
| **Events & People** | |
| **Issues & Themes** | |
| **Feeling:**<br>**General -**<br>**Self -**<br>**Others -** | |
| **Wants**<br>**Achievements** | |
| **Title:** | |

sights, sounds, and smells, too; watch and listen for them to all unfold before your closed eyes, take them all to heart, and be thankful for whatever does come to your consciousness. Then use all of your experience, your innocence, disillusionment, and wisdom, to write what you deeply feel from recalling those key moments of your life.

## The Unique Moment of Your Birth

> The character of a child is already plain, even in its mother's womb. Before I was born my mother was in great agony of spirit and in a tragic situation. She could take no food except iced oysters and champagne. If people ask me when I began to dance I reply, "In my mother's womb, probably as a result of the oysters and champagne—the food of Aphrodite."[15]

Each of us is born into a unique historical, social, cultural, familial, and parental moment. All of these factors merge to create a point in time that determines a large part of who we will become. What was going on in the world, your community, your family when you were being born? Was there anything unusual about your birth, any family stories told about your birth, that add significance or humor to the unique moment of your birth?

A little research into the historical moment of your birth might prove fascinating. What historical events or social issues and trends were current at the time of your birth? Did they have any impact on your life as you see it today? What was going on in your parents' lives when you were born? Which of these factors has had the greatest influence on who you are today? Write a story about these important events or influences in a flowing, conversational narrative that explains why and how they have had their impact on you.

A woman, born on December 25, 1943, to an unwed seventeen-year old, wrote about her birth in the form of a letter to the mother she never knew, but who had given her the nickname, Star:

> My Dearest Willa,
> As you may know, I never sent you the letter I wrote a little over five years ago, introducing myself as your daughter. You died a few months before I found you. Your husband and children have generously shared with me their memories and all they can remember of what you told them about me. Your having shared that information with them tells me a great deal about where my own strength and courage have come from.
> You would be pleased to know that I am in graduate school. David said you were always self-conscious about not completing high school. It is because of one of my courses that I am writing this letter. We are to describe as much as possible our own birth and circumstances surrounding that event.

I am happy to say I have a much clearer picture of that day than I did five years ago. I've tried several times to tell the story but I sound as if I'm talking about someone else's life. I realized the thoughts of you on the day of my birth made me feel very sad. Finally, when I began to write again, the words came out in the form of a letter.

I imagine at seventeen, you must have been feeling very frightened and alone—especially since it was Christmas time. I am curious to know why you chose Mercy Hospital since you were not Catholic. Was it because of my father? [Your old friend] Bunny told me that his family forbade the marriage because of their religion and implied there were feelings about social status. She said he was handsome and either an officer or an engineer in the merchant marines. She said you loved him but he went to sea soon after hearing about me and you never saw him again. You must have been feeling a tremendous sense of loss and abandonment. Maybe you chose Mercy Hospital because you knew you would need to return to work right after I was born and you knew I would be cared for by the nuns, at least for a few months. Did you ever get to hold me?

From what your family and friends have told me about you, it must have been a very difficult decision for you to finally place me for adoption. It was three years before you finally signed the papers. When I became a mother myself, I knew from a place inside that it must have been terribly difficult for you. We had a rough beginning, didn't we? I'm sure for a while, it must have seemed like just the two of us against the world.

It took me a long time and much soul searching before I had the courage to look for you. I wanted to meet the person I had secretly thought about and even longed for as an ally when things were less than perfect. I wanted to let you know I was having a good life. I am sure from what I have learned about you that you suffered from your decision far more than I ever did. For me, it was a new beginning. You set me free to live my own life and I am extremely grateful to you. My only regret is that I never got to tell you in person.

Love always,
Star *

Even though she still has many unanswered questions, the experience of putting them all down in a clear and organized form, and expressing many unvoiced feelings at the same time, has allowed a sense of completion that would not have been possible otherwise.

### A Core Childhood Experience

I can remember, at the age of five, being told that childhood was the happiest period of life (a blank lie, in those days). I wept inconsolably, wished I were dead, and wondered how I should endure the boredom of the years to come."[16]

Think back to your childhood years, from your earliest memories to about age twelve, and let all the important, crucial experiences flow through your mind as if they were a newsreel. Think about what it is that makes these experiences important to you. Focus on one experience for awhile, the one that stood out the most as they all flowed by, and recall as many details as you can about that one. Think of this event, experience, or memory, even if it is a series of events somehow interconnected, as having a beginning, a middle, and an end. Write your thoughts down in note form first, if necessary, then compose a narrative using the style that is most comfortable to you describing the experience, its impact on your life, and what you learned from this experience.

Childhood is many things to different people. For some, it may be the happiest period of life; for others it can be horrible. Mine was somewhere in the middle. It definitely was not horrible, but I've had my happiest times later in life. What follows is an example of how childhood can be quite devastating, but, with the perspective of hindsight and a deeper under-standing of life, we can actually make more sense of childhood later in life than we did when we were living it:

My parents were not what you would call the typical mom and dad. No, our house was nothing like Ward and June Cleever's. My mother didn't wear pearls to dinner or keep the house immaculate. My father didn't read the *Wall Street Journal* or smoke a pipe. The truth of the matter was that mother preferred long skirts and sandals to pearls and my father rarely read anything other than the *TV Guide*. They were about as different from the Cleevers and from each other as an elephant and jelly doughnut.

But I was happy as I could be at six. I had my own room and a pink canopy bed and more toys than I could ever play with. My world consisted of Ms. Zackatanski's first grade class, playing, and Josie and the Pussycats. I was oblivious to everything that went on around me. I wasn't "politically aware" or anything. I couldn't name the president. I didn't even realize that my parents were fighting.

One night, my parents woke me up in the middle of the night. It was probably only around 9:30, but when you go to bed at 8:00, it sure feels late. Both parents walked into my room and nudged me awake. I think my father mentioned something about a "family meeting." He carried me into the living room and sat down with me on his lap. My mother stood about three feet away facing us.

"Rebecca, we're going to have a little family meeting," she said. I thought this was really odd because we had never had a "family meeting" before. The biggest decision we ever made as a family—or at least one I was consulted on—was whether or not to get pepperoni on our pizza. It was also odd because my brother wasn't present for this "family meeting." Granted, at the time he was only two, but a family member nonetheless.

My father hugged me, which was something that usually did not happen on a regular basis. I knew that whatever they had to tell me was going to be a biggie. My father kept kissing me, and my mother mumbled something like, "Oh sure, kiss her now. You never bothered before."

My father started, "Sometimes things happen, and mommies and daddies stop loving one another—"

"—but that doesn't mean that they stop loving their children—"

"—Mommy and I love you and Kenny very, very much—"

"—and we always will—"

"—even if we don't love each other anymore—"

"—so your father won't be living here after tomorrow."

I didn't really listen to what they were saying, after all, it was late and I was still half asleep. They kept interrupting each other, each thinking they were saying it better, more sensitive. It all seemed pretty stupid to me and I could not understand why they would wake me for this. It never occurred to me that my parents ever loved each other, so what was the big deal if they stopped? And of course they loved me and Kenny, why wouldn't they? Why would I ever think that they would stop? I didn't pay any attention to the "your father won't be living here after tomorrow" line. I thought I heard wrong. I remember thinking that my parents were very, very weird.

"So do you understand what your father and I are saying?" my mother asked sheepishly. I then realized that my mother had been referring to him as "your father" instead of "Daddy" for some time now. I nodded my head and she said, "Okay, family meeting is over. You can go back to bed now, sweetie." I hopped off my father's lap and started walking to my room. My father then said, "I have to say this. Rebecca, this isn't Daddy's idea, I wanted to work this out with Mommy, but she just won't listen and—"

"George!" my mother yelled, and then she just gave him this look. Even at six, I knew that if looks could kill, my father would have been dead meat.

The next day, I woke up without really remembering the family meeting. I sat at the breakfast table, like I always did, but this time there were only three settings. My little brother was busy eating Cheerios with his hands, my mother was reading the paper. I looked around the room. Something was not right and I couldn't put my finger on it. Something was missing. And then it hit me. I ran over to the hutch and started screaming "Where is he!"

Let me backtrack a little. A few weeks earlier, my mother decided that it was a good idea if I had a few pet goldfish. She bought me a big round fish bowl and bright red gravel and I picked out three goldfish. I don't remember what two of their names were because they died within a day. The survivor I named Harold because, as I told my mother, "He looked like a Harold," although I can't remember ever knowing a Harold from which to compare my goldfish to.

For about a week, I fed Harold and talked to Harold and helped my mother clean Harold's fish bowl. And then I just sort of forgot about Harold. It then became solely my mother's job to care for my fish. I figured it was the least she could do considering it was her idea to get goldfish in the first place.

So here I was, in my fatherless kitchen, screaming away.

"Where is he Mommy? Where is he!"

"Sweetie, we told you last night that your father wasn't going to live here anymore —"

"Not Daddy! Where's my Harold!"

My mother had a real concerned look on her face. Kenny just kept on eating Cheerios with his fingers. "Rebecca, I told you last week that Harold died, don't you remember? I asked you if you wanted to flush him, and you told me to do it."

I just kept on screaming. "But Mommy! He didn't know! He didn't know that I loved him! I didn't get a chance to say goodbye! He doesn't know that I love him!"

My mother scooped me up into her arms and hugged me tight while I cried. "He knows, sweetie, he knows."

Looking back now, I know that my trauma was over my father and not my goldfish, but I didn't know that then. Harold could not have picked a better time to kick the bucket, because he taught me a valuable lesson. He taught me you can never say "I love you" too often. He taught me to appreciate what I have now, while it's here and not when it's gone. I think my mother suggested getting goldfish just for this reason—she knew what death, either physical or symbolic, teaches.

Over the past fifteen years since my parents' divorce, I've had like twenty different goldfish named Harold. They all die and they all teach the same lesson. But you know what? It doesn't get any easier.


## A Crucial Adolescent or Adult Transition

I was a fourteen year old boy for thirty years.[17]


Let your memories roll back to your teenage years, then let the newsreel of those years flow ahead toward your adult years and on up to the present. Notice particularly those times when you moved from one status to another, from one mode of being to another. Watch yourself especially as you go through those transitions, as you turn the corner from one thing to the next. It could even be something more subtle like a change in the way you looked at things or yourself. You may be surprised at how many transitions you can recall from your adolescent and adult years, ones that may have been long forgotten. Pick one turning point or transition that really stands out for you now, and look at it in depth. Try to see and understand the process that occurred during this transition. What caused this shift in your life? What did the change involve? Write the story of this process, the impact it has had on your life, and what you learned from it, in a style that is most comfortable to you.

A time of transition is usually a time of significant growth in our lives. This is because leaving the familiar behind can be difficult, and the change itself usually presents formidable challenges. But when faced, they become the source of the new growth. One woman wrote about the time she and her husband built their new house, and the impact this had on their lives:

> When Jeff and I decided to build a house, I was so excited. Oh, the plans I had: jaccuzzi's, decks, a black-and-white modern kitchen, sunken tiled bathroom. Building a house was going to be great! Jeff and I were taking a big step, using all our savings for the American dream of owning a home to raise a family in.
>
> As the dream turned into reality, and finances entered the plans, oh well, so much for the jaccuzzi, sunken tub, deck, and black-and-white kitchen! A 36 x 28 cape was the result. Nothing fancy but a house design Jeff and I were both happy with, at least for awhile.
>
> Little did I know that building a home could also cause me to change my views about loving my husband. Deadlines, red tape and decision after decision made building our home a living hell! Jeff was exhausted, I was constantly frustrated and worried due to broken promises and a dwindling savings account. I mean, was this what security and love was all about—crying every night, getting in major fights over what size grates to use in the windows, and never having enough time to make well-thought-out, discussed decisions?
>
> As the levels of exhaustion and frustration increased, down went the level of compromising and caring in Jeff's and my relationship. Often I had feelings of jealousy as Jeff went out weekends and nights to work on the house. I would feel like the house was my enemy instead of my dream coming true.
>
> As I sat night after night exploring my feelings, everything started to fall into place. Not only was the house coming into form, but so too was my adult relationship with Jeff. I began to understand what being married was all about. I began to realize the amount of effort and work a relationship takes to keep it solid. I began to feel like I could share Jeff with other things—like working on the house. As jealousy left my thoughts, I started to understand and feel real love.
>
> Real love for me is a calm emotion. It is a feeling of inner trust and full commitment. As Jeff and I moved in, I realized I had changed. Even though I knew Jeff since 5th grade, our relationship was just beginning.

I think what caused this change was the fact that I had no choice in taking a "backseat" in Jeff's priorities for a while. Since I wasn't the most important thing in his life (on the surface), I had to think about what our love was to each other and give to Jeff my support for his work instead of feeling jealous. Then when I gave support, Jeff's reaction was so positive, I realized that I *was* the most important thing in his life. My opinion and caring made him feel loved and vice-versa.

So, when I finally understood that true love is deep and calm, I became less afraid of sharing Jeff. Things like having children and starting a family aren't scary to me anymore. I feel really good now about Jeff and our marriage. I must admit that often when we were building the house I wanted to give only when I could get, but through quiet self-exploration and later talks with Jeff now I just want to give. After all, isn't that what love is all about?!

There are many other exercises that can be used to help understand past experiences better, and how they fit within the whole picture of our lives. Here are four others you might want to try.

*A peak experience* is a moment or event that surprises you with a sense of heightened emotion and joy; it may mean accomplishing something you had never been able to before or gaining a feeling of power, wholeness, aliveness, or union. We all experience something like this sometime in our lives. It may signal a new beginning or turning point in your life. Think about the times in your life like this, and write a story about what happened, how it felt, what you thought, and how the experience changed you or what impact it had on you.

*A Nadir Experience* is the opposite of a peak experience. It is a low point in your life, and we all have these, too. Think of an experience (or circumstance) in your life that you see as one of disappointment or disillusionment; perhaps you see it as the worst experience you have ever had in your life. Write a story about this experience, describing what happened, who was involved, how it felt, and how it turned out. If you want to try something different, you could give this story a "happy" ending and see what that feels like.

*A Plateau Experience* differs from a peak experience in that your primary feeling is one of serenity, calmness, enjoyment, happiness, marveling, wondering, contemplating, or pleasantness. If you have had an experience like this, write about what this was like, how it felt, what and how it happened.

*A Personal Hero/ine* is someone we all have in our lives, too, someone who has had a powerful impact on us in some way. They may be a close relative, a friend, a stranger, or even someone we have never actually met. Whoever that person is, he or she has given us something very important and probably intangible (guidance, support, a vision) that has stayed with us for many years. First, just make a list of all your heroes and heroines, beginning with the earliest you can remember and moving up to the present. Then, choose one, maybe the most significant, and write a page or so describing your hero or heroine, what this person gave you, and why he or she is important to you.

## LOOKING INWARD

The whole process of writing autobiographically is one of looking inward. But we may not keep up with what is going on inside us often enough. With each passing year, we accumulate more and more stuff, more ideas, more experience, more troubles, and more joys. Yet if we are not careful, if we do not take stock of what we have, of what is going on in the present, we can lose sight of those things that may have come the hardest, stayed the longest, and are really the most important to us.

Or, if we focus too much on one thing, some part of our life may overshadow what it is that makes us a whole, real, living, human being. We have to be careful not to let one part become more important than the whole of who we are. It can be very helpful to reflect on the one or two most enduring things that really make us us, and enable us to be that whole human being.

It is very important to examine where we are, what we have, and what is going on in the present moment. This could tell us what our current feelings are, what is most important to us right now, or what it is that we are not thinking about that maybe we should be dealing with.

A little exercise to help with this process is called "Counting Your Blessings." We may not express our gratitude often enough for the things that we do have. We may not even really be aware of what we have to be thankful for. Reflect on your blessings, first making a list of all the good things you now have in your life, then go back and write a sentence or two about each one. You might also try weaving them together in a story that expresses what you are at this point grateful for in your life.

### Your Spiritual Self

> As I approach my eighty-fourth year, I find it interesting to reflect on what has made my life, even with its moments of pain, such an essentially happy one. I have come to the conclusion that the most important element in human life is faith. If God were to take away all his blessings: health, physical fitness, wealth, intelligence and leave me but one gift, I would ask for faith."[18]

Find your own place of quiet where you can relax and reflect deeply on the question: Who are you at your essence? Think back over the important experiences of your life. Is there a common thread that ties your life

together? Do you feel that you have a clear life theme? How do your actual
life experiences connect with your deepest dream for your life?

Think of the core of your life as what is spiritual. If everything around
you were to change at some point in your life, what would remain constant
within you? What concerns you the most in life? Whatever you come up
with, that is what holds your life together, gives you your greatest meaning,
and is also the essence of your spiritual self. Think about your own unique
spiritual quest, your quest for meaning and authenticity, from your birth to
the present. How did your spiritual self unfold? Are there gradual stages
or a key transformational experience that shaped your spiritual life?

Write the story of how you grew spiritually, of how you came to know
your spiritual self and become the core of who you are today. Then read
over what you have written, reflect on your words some more and, when
you are comfortable with what you have written, and that it really is you,
you might want to find someone close to you to share it with.

When we think about the evolution of our spiritual self, our task is to
focus on that one experience that in some dramatic way changed everything
for us, or on the series of events that gave us the spiritual awareness, or
sense of meaning, that we have now. One woman, now in her thirties,
sought the common thread from her childhood and adult years by focusing
on a key experience from when she was twenty-three:

> My deepest dream for myself is to freely be what I am to the greatest
> degree possible. I continually work toward this goal. My childhood experi-
> ences have made this quest vital to me. My early self was discouraged and
> hidden away to ensure survival. I never gave up seeking to be myself despite
> the strong influence of others who sought to destroy my individuality. My
> inner survival may have been due to a combination of stubbornness and a
> level of abuse which was not too great to overcome. Guilt and anxiety were
> the predominant feelings of my youth. In my mid-twenties I was no longer
> able to associate the guilt with any specific event. It was just a feeling I woke
> up with and lived with for a part of each day. The anxiety became so intense
> that I sought counseling. For the first time, I could identify and live by my
> own feelings. It took a while because I had been so carefully trained to deny
> my own emotions. I now relish the opportunity to know my true self.
>
> I have experienced a sense of oneness with everything. This is my spiritual
> experience, the proof I have that there is something beyond daily life. I clearly
> remember my first experience of oneness. I was twenty-three years old and
> recently divorced. I had been in therapy for about a year at the time. It
> occurred as I was driving my car to a friend's house. I came over a small hill
> and noticed the sun shining brightly over a rock at the side of the road.
> Suddenly everything felt right with the world. I had an intense feeling of
> pleasure and peace. But more importantly, I felt a part of everything, the sun,

the rock, the earth, and everything on it and beyond it. That was the most intense and incredible high I have ever experienced. Words do not do it justice. When I tried to capture the feeling it went away. I have experienced something similar on several occasions since but never as intensely. I have spoken to people who have had similar occurrences, which leads me to believe that this experience is universally possible. I wonder if this is the spiritual energy that religious people are seeking.

The experience of oneness has made death less frightening to me. If I am part of everything, then my death does not destroy me because I continue to be a part of everything that goes on. I have found at my core a deep sense of optimism that I will back. That does not mean that I will never meet misfortune or that I will not die. It simply means that whatever happens is as it should be. I like myself. I am unfolding as I should be. It's difficult at times. Keeping in touch with my own feelings and being honest with myself takes effort. I am more successful at some times than others.

I am not connected to a religious group. I do not like the rigidity that formal religion entails. I have never been able to accept the beliefs of one group or another as the only path to follow. I do believe the spiritual leaders such as Jesus, Buddha, Lao-Tse, and Mohammed were extraordinary and enlightened men. I do miss having a spiritual community. The idea of coming together with others to discuss spiritual questions and worship in a personal manner is appealing to me. I would like to eventually find such a community.

I am aware that there is much more to learn about my own spirituality. It's a process that I am experiencing and I feel confident that I am progressing as I should. I look forward to understanding my place in the world better. I love this opportunity to be alive. I appreciate sharing this life and my growth with those I love. I will continue my struggle to become myself.

## LOOKING AHEAD

> I never expected to have, in my sixties, the happiness that passed me by in my twenties.[19]

Moments of deep reflection about your past and present are always helpful. It is just as helpful to think deeply, sincerely, and openly about your future, keeping in mind that nothing in your present or past necessarily predetermines what is to come. It is up to you to bring about what you most want for yourself in the future. But you have to know what you really want first.

Thinking about possibilities without limiting yourself to what you have experienced in the past will keep your future open and make it a lot more exciting. There are bound to be changes and surprises ahead, everything won't be smooth, and you probably won't have full control over what does happen. The only nonsurprise in your future may be death, so that may not be such a difficult one after all. It is something that we can think realistically about because it is bound to happen. That fact may even help us and make it more important to think seriously about what we really want for ourselves *before* that happens.

Some of what lies ahead may even exceed your imagination. Twenty years ago I could never have anticipated all that has happened to me since then. And even if I let my fantasies run wild, I would still be surprised at what actually does come to be. The reason for thinking about our future, regardless of what actually happens, is that the more we think about it, the more we give ourselves opportunities to weigh different possibilities, the more accepting we will be of whatever does happen. Fantasy is often the mother of creativity. Life is unpredictable, yet our lives expand, blossom, and flourish as much as we allow them to!

The first of two exercises here uses a guided visualization to help you get in touch with your elder self so you have a better sense of who you will be in the future. The second helps you focus the vision you have for yourself for the future. There are three steps to successful visioning: knowledge, volition, and action. We have to really know what we want for ourselves, we have to really want what we want strongly and clearly enough, and we have to act so as to make happen what we want. I will say a little more about these three parts of visioning after the exercises and the examples of writing. For the visualization, it would be best if you had a friend read it to you, or tape it and play it back for yourself, when you are ready to do it. (The dots represent places you can pause.)

### Your Elder Self

Let's take a few moments for quiet reflection, to let your senses rest, and to find your own inner place of peace. . . .

Close your eyes, listen for the silence, feel the rhythm of your breathing, and enjoy its relaxing motion. . . .

Now, open your inner eye, to meet your elder self. . . .

Ahead of you lies a wonderful path; it could be in a meadow, on a mountain, or by the sea, wherever you are most drawn. . . .

It is a beautiful, warm day, you are walking on your soft, gentle trail. It has been there since the beginning of time. . . .

Soon, the path takes a turn into a comforting tunnel; this is a time tunnel, and you pass by many doors, some of the doors can take you back in time, and some ahead into the future. . . .

You come to a door that leads back to your childhood. You open that door and walk in. There your child self is waiting to greet you. Listen to what it has to say to you. . . .

Listen to what you have to say to your child self. . . .

After you have gotten acquainted again, invite your child self to come with you on a journey into the future. . . .

You enter the time tunnel again and walk, and walk. Finally you come to a door that leads to your elder self. You open the door, walk in, and the two of you greet your elder self. . . .

Listen to what your child self says to your elder self. Let them get to know each other, enjoy their interaction. . . .

What do you most want to ask your elder self? . . .

Listen to what your elder self has to say to you. What does your elder self want you to know about your life? . . .

What do you feel now from this meeting? . . . .

When you have said all that you want to say to each other, you are ready to leave the time tunnel, and begin your return back along your path. . . .

Take a few quiet moments now to be with yourself, to really feel what went on, and then write down what you discovered from this experience.

Timing can be a real key to having a visualization work well for you. And sometimes hard truths can become evident during a visualization. One woman had nearly lost her marriage earlier in the year. It was a very traumatic experience, but it had the positive effect of helping her learn acceptance. She had such a reaction to the visualization that she had to get up and leave the room while everyone else was still writing down their thoughts from it. The tears just welled up from inside and poured out. Later she wrote:

> It seems as though my entire life has been spent rushing. I am constantly in a hurry to find time to make time to have a break in the pace at work; to do something with the family; to spend an hour on myself in exercise class; to knit; to go to school. If I continue this way my fear is that I will miss the more important parts in life. The paradox is that since I can remember, it has been important to me that I do not turn sixty only to have regrets about how I lived my life. This is precisely what drives me to try and do so much!
>
> The visualization we did really drove it home. I genuinely look forward to growing old. During the visualization I really couldn't imagine myself living long enough to have an elder self. I literally did not at that instant believe that I could continue to live at this pace.
>
> It turns out that the visualization has had a profound impact on my way of thinking. I am still deeply committed to living a life I can be proud of. However, it occurs to me that there is more than one way to do that. Maybe rushing to do everything and making more time to do more is not as effective as it once was. The things that are important to me now have changed. I don't want to rush anymore. I would like to be at peace with myself.
>
> Greater acceptance and tolerance will enable me to meet the future with more ease. I would like to relax more and begin to let things happen to me

instead of always making things happen. I want to start conserving some of that energy to use enjoying the simple things. I want to live the rest of my life gracefully.

When I spoke with her almost two years later, she still referred to that experience as life-changing. She said, "As long as I live, that experience will stay with me. It was that voice telling me: 'You can't run away.' "

### Envisioning Your Life

Find a quiet place for reflection. Think about your own ideal for the life you have yet to live. What is your vision of your future? Suppose you could live the future you want. The way you see your life from today forward may determine the way your life will turn out in the end. How would that affect the way you think about the rest of your life? Dream, think about your purpose, try on different possibilities, envision the future you really want for yourself.

A vision may start out vague, but as you add your secret dreams, let it take shape, decide it is something you really want, and follow your vision, it can become reality. What would your life be like if it could be what you most want it to be? What if you grew with every crisis, as well as with every opportunity? What else do you seek in life? What contributions do you most want to make to others, to the world? What commitments are most important to you? What inspires you? What promises to yourself would keep you going? What would make your life complete when you die? Imagine being delighted with and appreciative of *everything* that happens in your life.

Think about these things and give yourself time to determine and decide for yourself what you really want from the rest of your life. Imagine yourself five, ten, twenty, or thirty years from now as you would most like to be, having done the things you most want to do. What is the thing you've done that is most satisfying to you? What contribution have you made to the world that makes you the proudest? What is your greatest source of happiness? How would you have to change your life from today onward to make this happen? Weave what you come up with into a story about the rest of your life that reveals your personal truth and you as the designer of a life you can feel good about.

In visioning our future, it is helpful to remember that there will be losses along with the gains. Some of those losses are predictable and others are not. It is up to you to choose what you want to focus on in your future.

One woman, in her mid-thirties, worked hard in recovery, and wanted to help others discover the freedom she had found. She entered graduate school in counseling, and wrote about her work in substance abuse counseling and research as an eighty-four year old looking back on her accomplishments, adding a light touch to a very serious matter:

> We now understand the significance of the connection between the physical, psychological, and spiritual aspects of addiction as recognized by the founders of AA and researched by many over the decades. The most exciting finding for me was the discovery of an innate "hole in the middle" which all human beings are born with. Through massive longitudinal research, huge population surveys, and major efforts within close spiritual communities, we have come to recognize and accept this common denominator of humanity. Some of us call it a "God Hole." It is an existential void, which humans are driven all of their lives to keep satisfactorily full. We know that we cannot exist if this hole is empty. It must be filled with something, or we will die—perhaps a slow physical death, but a very quick emotional and spiritual death. Humans will not survive in a state of spiritual and emotional emptiness.
>
> Over the years, we have identified many ways people use to fill this hole. Drugs (particularly alcohol) and food have been the most common substances used, but many other negative self-destructive behaviors have emerged to do the job. I have observed people filling the hole with sex, abusive treatment of other people, power, manipulation, an increasing lust for technology, and many more. Since we have clearly identified "the Hole," we have been able to bring new hope to the addiction field.
>
> Well, as you can see, my interests have grown and evolved from some very concrete methods of working with individual substance abusers into a larger, global concern for a common human emptiness. In my remaining years, I will continue to encourage people to meet together, reach out to one another, and reflect their Creator to one another.

Writing about ourselves in the future is like a life preview. It gives us a pretty clear sense of what we can expect, what we want to happen, and what can happen. It may even make us think seriously about the idea that anything we can think, we can do. Thinking about what we really want, and giving our repressed desires or unexpressed dreams a voice and a shape on paper, makes them conscious and helps us plan to be what we want to be. Admitting to ourselves what we want makes our thoughts about our future clear and, even more important, real and worthy of our attention. Knowing what we want to be doing five or ten years from now gives us a sense of what will be necessary to bring it about. That's the knowledge part of visioning our future. We have to first dare to define and give direction to our vision.

That's what allowed one undergraduate to write, "I think now that I have a better idea of what I want out of life, and where my priorities should lie. You have given me a lot to look forward to, and I will welcome my future, no matter what it may bring." When we know what we want, we are a third of the way there.

Looking ahead also tells us that our life is not over. Every day there is still something else that we can do or be with our lives, when we are not writing about them. The second step is even more important. A strong desire is required to be able to move on from the point of knowing what we know. We have to will ourselves to be able to see ourselves in the way we know we want ourselves to be. As one woman wrote, "I see myself engaged in the lives of others, assisting them towards emotional and educational growth. I see myself as one who creates 'safe' environments that encourage self-disclosure and sharing without fear. I see myself as a tool or resource to be used by others who seek liberation from their pasts or from their own mediocrity and stagnation." This is the *volition* part of visioning our future.

Our mind may set off on its own to bring about what it knows and really wants, with or without us. But to take less of a chance, we could begin to act as if what we really want is about to happen or is happening. To do what we want is the surest way to bring about the future we want. We need to respond to the call we hear from within us by some kind of action. When we know our dream, our vision, it is time to be fairly practical and take the steps necessary to make it happen. Believing in our vision is one thing, living it is another. With a vision, we are also usually given the means to fulfill it. A plan of action with specific steps is what will move us closer and closer to our vision.

This is what the woman in her thirties did, who wrote about her accomplishments as an eighty-four-year old. She knew she wanted to leave her old career behind, become trained as a counselor, and help others leave their problems with alcohol behind. So she took the first step by enrolling in the counseling program. The next steps were in her vision of her future: she got her degree, got a counseling job that would give her time for her research interests, left her old career, worked in substance abuse, did research, discovered "the hole in the middle," and wrote about it all as if it had already happened. Writing about things as if they are happening can be as important as living as if they are happening. Both are the *action* part of visioning.

Knowing the future we want, willing it, and consciously directing our energies toward bringing it about, is how projecting our life into the future works for our benefit. It is also a very important part of our life story, because following this three-step process can give our life story the ending that we will be happiest with.


With all of the writing you have done in response to these exercises, you now have many stories that together make up the story of your life. You can be sure it is an impressive and important document. Putting the pieces together as a flowing narrative may be a matter of filling in the gaps or adding some linking or transitional sentences to smooth the shift from one exercise to the next. You also have a head start on telling your personal myth because you will be able to recognize how the sacred pattern has expressed itself in your life.

You have also re-created yourself. You have created a self that you know more about now than you did before you started writing about yourself. You are much closer to knowing and becoming your true self, the self you can love and accept in spite of probably having had many painful experiences in life. Autobiographical writing is transformational; through it we feel ourselves moving closer to what we can potentially be, and this is one of our greatest joys.

## NOTES

1. Frank, *The diary of a young girl*, p. 211.
2. Hillman, A note on story, pp. 43–45.
3. John Kotre and Elizabeth Hall, *Seasons of life*, pp. 128–129
4. Hillesum, *An interrupted life*, pp. 44, 46, 59, 92, 219.
5. Guthrie, My oughtabiography, pp. 8–9.
6. Dillard, *The writing life*, p. 75.
7. Goldberg, *Writing down the bones*, p. 29.
8. Baldwin, *Life's companion*, p. 17.
9. Rico, *Writing the natural way*, p. 136; Baldwin, *Life's companion*, pp. 51, 151; Welty, *One writer's beginnings*, p. 111.
10. Welty, *One writer's beginnings*, p. 111.
11. Ueland, *If you want to write*, pp. 63–70.
12. Zinsser (ed.), *On writing well*.
13. The following sources would also be helpful for autobiographical writing: Adams, *Journal to the self*; Baldwin, *Life's companion*; Birren, The best of all stories, Daniel, *How to write your own life story*; Goldberg, *Writing down the bones*; Gould, *The writer in all of us*; Hughes, *Writing for the inner self*; Rico, *Writing the natural way*; Santa-Maria, *Growth through Meditation*; Solly and Lloyd, *Journey notes*; and Wakefield, *The story of your life*.
14. Kierkegaard, *The living thoughts of Kierkegaard*, p. 25.
15. Duncan, *My life*, quoted in Sampson, *The Oxford book of ages*, p. 3.
16. Russell, *On education*, quoted in Sampson, *The Oxford book of ages*, p. 16.
17. Mickey Rooney quoted in Sampson, *The Oxford book of ages*, p. 38 .
18. Kennedy, *Times to remember*, quoted in Sampson, *The Oxford book of ages*, p. 157.
19. C. S. Lewis, quoted in Sampson, *The Oxford book of ages*, p. 116.

# 5

## *Universalizing Your Story: Personal Mythmaking*

I have now undertaken, in my eighty-third year, to tell my personal myth.[1]

Your personal myth takes you right into the sacred realm of your life. It helps you explore those elements of your life that have made you authentically you. It gets you in touch with your soul and with everyone else at the same time. Your personal myth has the ring of "Once upon a time...." It opens you to the timelessness and universality of your story and transports you to that sacred place in your own life where you find a deep connection to other lives where past, present, and future merge.

A personal myth is the story of our life that focuses on the experiences, motifs, and emotions most common to other human beings. It is told within the framework of the sacred pattern of beginning, conflict, and resolution, or separation, initiation, and return. It connects our lives to those who have gone before us by conveying what is most important and meaningful to us, especially the ultimate concerns, events, feelings, and beliefs that have directed our growth. We can tell our personal myth, a series of events or experiences connected by a common thread, in any style we are comfortable with. Since our personal myth follows a pattern that repeats itself often in our lives, we will probably have many personal myths or expressions of the three-part pattern making our complete life story.

In preparing to write your personal myth, you will be trying to gain access to your *mythological voice*.[2] This is the voice of your soul, the voice that is in touch with your deepest values and beliefs, your most universally human experiences. This is the voice that communicates between your soul and your mind, carrying information about the lasting, eternal world for you to use in the everyday world. It is really very important to be aware of this exchange and to nurture this ongoing communication with your mythological voice on a daily basis in order to keep yourself in touch with your deepest level of consciousness, what Jung called the collective unconscious.

This means that you will have to search for and acknowledge *all* parts of your experience. Your personal myth is the story of how you have overcome formidable obstacles in your way. It may include symbolic expressions of having gone through a "dark night of the soul" or having traversed treacherous terrain in order to come to some new understanding of yourself. But because of these difficulties that you acknowledge, your personal myth is primarily an adventure, the great adventure of your life! Your personal myth is the story of how you become whole, how you reach your potential, how you overcome your challenges to achieve transformation.

As far as I can determine, Jung was the first to designate an autobiography a "personal myth." Of course, all the classical myths were "personal" myths in a sense too, but they were told or written by someone other than the "god" or "goddess" whose life they are about. They are more like biographical myths.

Jung's autobiography, *Memories, Dreams, Reflections*, abounds with archetypal/sacred images and examples of how the three-part mythic pattern played itself out in his life. His childhood, youth, and adulthood were full of the transformative motifs of myth, like calls to adventure, protective figures, thresholds to cross, the withdrawal inward, trials and ordeals, rebirths, and much giving back to others. These are some of the more important archetypes and motifs that make up the three-part pattern that we will be exploring here to create your personal myth. They are the kinds of archetypal experiences that everyone can find among their own life experiences when they are familiar with them.

Jung said in his autobiography, "What we are to our inward vision . . . can only be expressed by way of myth."[3] He means that at our essence, we are like all other human beings. Myth is a precise way of expressing the universals of life: it shows us that the same events, experiences, and feelings we have experienced have been part of the human experience forever. Myth captures the essence of our lives; our personal myth captures the types of events and feelings that are familiar to others.

To write about your life in this mythic, archetypal mode is to take up an eternal quest, to give your life an inner power that we all yearn for. This is the power that leads to transformation. And this transformation leads to a selfless desire to contribute something of our own to the whole of which we are a part.

## KEYS TO THE PERSONAL MYTH

Personal mythmaking is following a road map for navigating life's transitions. It describes in detail the journey we embark upon to achieve a transformation of character, of status, and of personality. The process that this transformation follows is timeless and universal. Its pattern is set. It hasn't changed over time. It is very unlikely that it ever will.

The world's myths and folktales are built upon this same pattern. Cultural traditions may vary in regard to social custom and laws. But tradition is remarkably uniform when it comes to the progress of the human spirit. Some cultural tales isolate certain themes or elements in the pattern and enlarge them. Others may skip over some of the smaller elements of the pattern. But in the endless tellings and retellings of traditional stories, the core pattern is always evident. And in the close examination of a life, that same pattern is evident, as well.

Mythological figures, themes, and motifs are not just products of our unconscious mind; they are the essence of our waking moments as well. Experiencing archetypal themes in our life is one of the purposes of our life, because they are agents of transformation.

To live the mythic pattern is to experience the total range of the spiritual life. The person who has this timeless, transformative experience and is able to share it in some way with others is a real *spiritual* hero or heroine.

The spiritual sense of the pattern is evident in the initiation rites of traditional societies, where the child dies to its childness and is reborn a responsible adult. This is not only a universal psychological process that we all must undergo at some point, in some way, in our lives; it is also a sacred transformation, a spiritual experience that brings with it a new level of commitment and responsibility to others.[4]

The way of living the archetype is really thoroughly known, for all the heroes and heroines that have gone before us have illustrated the pattern of spiritual renewal. But in order for them to become renewed, they have had to undergo a highly significant series of trials and ordeals. This is most evident in initiation rites, which are never easy experiences. The importance of these personal ordeals should not be lost on us today. We see more and more these days, how the horrendous sufferings and tests that people have endured in their personal and interpersonal lives come to the surface and demand attention.

These sufferings are the reason for the existence of the remarkably popular twelve-step programs. The way to both recovery and spiritual growth is through recognizing our pain and shortcomings and making the conscious effort to release ourselves from the trap of their bondage.

The process of acknowledging our condition and consciously striving to go beyond that to a new status mirrors precisely what has happened forever in mythological realms, too. The sacred pattern in all of its various forms carries within it a test of courage, which gives us the opportunity to summon from within what is necessary to achieve a transformation of consciousness.

The traditional initiation rite—the mythic quest—and twelve-step programs each, in essence, brings about an alteration of inner awareness and a change in the way we perceive our own self. This is what allows us to utilize our sufferings for not only the psychological transition from one level of maturity to the next but also for a spiritual renewal as well.

Living the sacred pattern (whether in a traditional ritual or in everyday life) and personal mythmaking both mean learning to see the positive values in what appear to be negative moments. We are often challenged and tested significantly, but rarely beyond our capacity. Successfully making it through the entire process of transformation is like getting to the upper range of human potential. This possibility for transformation is built into the blueprint within us all.

It is important to note that personal mythmaking may be a somewhat different experience for different people, only sometimes depending on whether you are female or male. As discussed in chapter 3, there is one sacred pattern, or blueprint, that fits all. However, there are two ways of approaching or experiencing the pattern. These two ways are not necessarily predetermined by gender. First, there is the providing, taking-in way of transformation, then the seeking, going-out way of transformation. Either way can work, and be just as effective, for any of us. More to the point is Maureen Murdock's view that the heroine's journey begins with "separation from the feminine" and ends with "integration of masculine and feminine."[5]

Over the past twenty-five years, I have found that what Joseph Campbell calls the "monomyth,"[6] is the most effective framework for telling my personal myth and helping others to tell theirs. The monomyth is a single, three-part story made up of archetypes and motifs from countless myths, legends, and folktales. It expresses the common pattern followed by all the hero myths of the world. With it we can readily recognize and identify the same archetypal themes in our own life experiences.

I have used this approach with students, women and men, ranging from twenty to seventy years of age. All have been able to successfully identify, and thereby give deeper meaning to, their personal experiences that reflect part or all of this mythic pattern. What I offer here is a way of writing mythologically that draws upon Campbell's classic *Hero With a Thousand Faces*. I have made adaptations to the mythic pattern he describes so it might be better understood in relation to our lives today.

You can start with some of the same events and experiences you may have already written about as part of your autobiography and see what part or parts might fit within this pattern. It may help not only to become more familiar with our own life story but those of other people as well, since that will make us even more familiar with the universal motifs that appear in peoples' lives.

There are three steps in preparing to write your personal myth. First, personal mythmaking requires becoming more familiar with the three major archetypes of the sacred pattern found in story, myth, ritual, and many developmental theories, as described in Exhibit 3.1. Each of the three steps—separation, initiation, and return—is an archetype by itself, and together they provide a clear overview of the entire process. We need to know what each part contributes to the whole of the process of birth, death, and rebirth. This is what the exercises and worksheets that follow will do for us.

Second, personal mythmaking also includes becoming familiar with each of the motifs, or smaller elements, within the three main parts of the larger archetype. These motifs are illustrated in great detail in *Hero With a Thousand Faces*. A summary of these motifs, with their contemporary counterparts, are offered in the next section, along with the accompanying exercises.

Third, personal mythmaking consists of looking over our own life experiences and feelings to determine how they reflect the ageless archetypal experiences and feelings of the pattern. This means understanding that our own life experiences can and do mirror archetypal experiences, those human experiences and themes that have recurred throughout time and in every setting. The two examples of contemporary personal myths that follow will help you identify your own archetypal experiences.

The actual writing work of personal mythmaking consists of three steps, as well. First, each of the three main parts contains an exercise that focuses on questions designed to help you recall specific events and experiences that fall within the archetypal experiences of that part. Second, a worksheet is provided where you can place your own personal motifs and what they mean to you in the context of the archetypes and motifs of the mythic pattern. Third, a writing exercise is used for each part to help you turn the rough notes identifying your personal motifs (paralleling the mythic motifs) into a flowing narrative of three parts that becomes your personal myth.

You will be trying to determine to what degree your own life experience follows this mythic pattern. Personal mythmaking is a process of self-discovery that adds perspective, depth, and connectedness to your sense of being. Personal mythmaking can be an extremely powerful and personally significant experience.

The process of writing a personal myth is not therapy, but it can be therapeutic. What usually qualifies as therapy is what someone else helps us discover or accomplish with us. Personal mythmaking, like journal writing or autobiography, is what we do on our own. It probably qualifies as self-therapy. I have thought of personal mythmaking as *"my*therapy,"

Exhibit 5.1
An Outline of Archetypes and Motifs for Personal Mythmaking

## I. SEPARATION

1.  *Call to Adventure*
    The first sign of a new phase of life unfolding; we can either go with it, or hold on to the familiar world.
2.  *Assistance*
    After we enter a new, unknown realm, we find that we are being protected and come to feel we are being guided along our way.
3.  *The Initial Challenge*
    We get a warning of impending danger as we move deeper into new realms, but as we proceed, the danger fades.
4.  *Retreat*
    We find ourselves in a time of withdrawal, of turning inward or reflecting on our situation, and being cut off from the world in some way.

## II. INITIATION

1.  *Greater Challenges*
    As we continue on, we are faced with more difficult tasks and struggles that we must deal with and overcome.
2.  *Further Assistance*
    We meet someone or something, maybe even a new aspect of our inner selves, that helps us in some way, or gives us a glimpse of what is possible and what is to come.
3.  *Temptation*
    Exposure to something different tests our personal values and standards, and we become clearer what our true standards are.
4.  *Renewal and Rebirth*
    Fear dissolves, we die to the old, and are reborn, more than we were. Yet, with our full potential within reach, and looking to the role of guiding others, we know that we are still quite vulnerable.

## III. RETURN

1.  *Responsibility Accepted or Denied*
    We either deny, are prevented, or return to the world. If we survive the impact of returning, we want to give something back of what we have been given.
2.  *Living Consciously*
    In consciously knowing the struggle of having lived in both the temporal and the eternal worlds, the personal and the collective, at the same time, and that others may not understand our experience, we begin to find our own balance, recognizing that we are always in the process of becoming, that we are interdependent with others, and that we are peace with the way things are.

because it is what I can do from myself, by myself, and for myself. It is a change that occurs as a result of the new way I see my own life experience through the perspective of myth. I do *"my*therapy" by closely examining what has happened in my life and then relating that to what has happened in the lives of the gods and goddesses of ancient time. And, just as important, because I do it for me, the result also benefits those around me. I like to think of personal mythmaking as a means to achieve a greater degree of our potentiality.

## AN OVERVIEW OF THE PERSONAL MYTH

As seen in Exhibit 3.1, the pattern we will be using for personal mythmaking can be made to appear quite simple or very complicated. It helps to really understand its most basic form first, that of beginning, muddle, and resolution. Every life, and most sequences of events in our lives, has a beginning point that is different from what preceded that; following this is a period that is different from the first, which creates some kind of conflict or problem to be solved in order to regain the balance lost; the next period consists of what happens when that conflict is resolved in some way and how we then carry on in our lives.

This is exactly what happens in initiation rites when we are removed from the familiar and thrust into an unknown realm; we have to make it on our own and discover the mysteries of the sacred world that have made us who we are, and then return to our community to take on our new responsibilities in life.

It is not much of a leap from here to the departure-initiation-return variation of the mythic pattern described by Campbell. He says the mythological adventure of the hero is a magnification of the formula represented in rites of passage.

A close look at the archetypes and motifs within the three-part mythic pattern shows us that it expresses the deepest of human emotions and needs while giving life some of its most profound meaning. The mythic pattern, broken down by archetype or motif, represents the awakening of the self, the beginning of transformation, the awareness of being guided, approaching the danger with courage, withdrawing and turning inward, purifying the self, discovering and utilizing one's hidden capacities, expanding one's consciousness, dying to the old and being reborn to the new, realizing a serenity and compassion, accepting both joy and sorrow, and remaining assured while giving of oneself freely.

This means that at different times in our lives we find ourselves guided through the ordinary world and into what feels like a realm of wonders, where we encounter formidable challenges and emerge renewed, able to bestow a gift of some kind upon others. This is a process of letting go of one status, acquiring a new status that expands our awareness and abilities, and then living in this new status with a greater impact on others. When we become conscious of this experience, we realize that we are the hero or heroine of our own life story and that we have our own personal version of this myth to tell.

Although we will be working the three parts of the pattern separately, it helps to get first a clearer sense of how the parts fit together as a whole and, through two examples, a sense of what a personal myth looks like.

It is especially important to note that the motifs in the outline in Exhibit 5.1 are given as universal, but they may not be experienced in the exact same order by everyone. Some may be experienced out of sequence, and some not at all. But if you take a close look at the following motifs, you will see that they represent a repetition of the basic pattern of crisis followed by victory. Each repetition of the crisis/victory minipattern is a variation on the previous one and builds upon the lessons that each earlier experience of the minipattern teaches us. When we look back on them in the end, each repetition of crisis/victory flows together, making a "good story."

The period of time a personal myth can cover in a person's life varies greatly; it depends on which events in your life you see as most transformative for you. One woman framed her personal myth from the time of the break up of her marriage to the time a few years later when she got a new job where she was able to share more of herself with others. She was not expecting her call to adventure when it came; she desperately tried to hold on to the role she knew best at that time—wife and mother. But her marriage disintegrated and with it her sense of identity. The thought of living unmarried in a married world was terrifying to her and fraught with unknown dangers. She felt as if her present and future life was out of control. Close friends urged her to seek a counselor. She did and the counselor became indispensable in her attempt to put the pieces back together. Over the next few months, she began to see that she would survive and emerge a stronger person. She dealt with other struggles like court appearances, financial hardships, supporting her children. She faced these, but also withdrew into herself and avoided situations where she would have to explain herself to others.

She met and overcame each ordeal along the way; she grew stronger and more confident as she drew upon her inner resources and slayed the dragons of pride, stubbornness, and fear. She felt her old self dying, even as others reassured her and as she was flooded with new sensations. She risked more than before, enjoyed it, felt acutely sensitive to subtleties as never before, and became an avid observer of other people and their relationships. It was as if a film had been dropped from her eyes.

She knew there was much work yet to be done to make sense of the turbulent events of the preceding months before she would be able to fully return to her family, friends, and work. She did begin to see the meaning in what had happened and what she was doing, and that her married friends did not really want to hear the details of her failed marriage. She needed to find friends whose circumstances were more like hers. A powerful force was pulling her back to her home state, so she moved back, and a new job as an admissions counselor in higher education has given her enormous satisfaction and fulfillment. She draws upon her own life experience and struggles in making a difference in the lives of the people she works with.

The second example of a personal myth covers a time span in another woman's life from when she began pre-med studies during college to when she completed her master's degree in gerontology, fifty years later. Her call to adventure was deciding to pursue a career in medicine, the profession followed by seven of her paternal ancestors. She got her bachelor's degree in biology, magna cum laude, but soon found herself engaged to another pre-med student, who said one doctor in the family would be sufficient and it would be he! They were married in July 1940, he finished medical school, and she worked as a secretary-lab technician to a biology professor, who became her mentor. Soon, her husband was shipped to the South Pacific, as an Army lieutenant, leaving her alone in her solitude with a five-month-old infant and pregnant with the second of their three daughters.

Her trials became even more pronounced as she continued to submerge her aspirations of a career in medicine to the duties of wife and mother. Temptations arose to threaten the marriage, but it was renewed and made stronger. The years passed, their daughters grew and went off on their own, and she became active in the community. She and her husband had begun their ideal retirement, but in that first year her husband died of cardiac arrest. She felt surrounded by a mist, having to take care of everything and make the transition from wife to widow to woman. She turned inward, went to church, and started a master's degree in adult education and gerontology with the encouragement of both her pastor and her therapist. She began to pursue her studies without guilt and with great vigor. Then, on Ash Wednesday, at a service of Penitence and Healing, she felt her rebirth through a transcendent experience. She surrendered her life to God, gave up her drinking, and committed herself to helping her peers through grief counseling. Now, at seventy-two, having completed one master's, she is beginning another in divinity.

Before going through the three-part process of writing your personal myth, you may want to recall a period in your life that reflects this pattern of beginning, muddle, and resolution, to get a sense of how your story will flow as a whole. Then you can work on the details of each part by doing the following exercises.

## PHASE ONE: SEPARATION

The separation phase of the mythic pattern involves a departure from one place to another or an inner separation that leads from one status to another.[7] In either case, it begins with a *Call to Adventure* that signals the beginning of a new life. In classic form, this might involve entering a dark forest, an underground kingdom, or, in the case of King Arthur and the Knights of the Round table, going off on a quest. In the fairytale, "The Frog Prince," passing a babbling brook becomes the scene and source of a dramatic transformation to follow. This motif means the carrier of destiny has arrived.

Numerous contemporary forms of this motif exist, which means ending one phase of life and beginning another. It could include leaving home, moving to a new area, divorce, beginning a new relationship, becoming pregnant, beginning college, beginning a career, becoming seriously ill, or being introduced to a new way of seeing things. In the twelve-step programs, the "call" could be accepting your powerlessness over your own situation and beginning the process of recovery (Step 1).

Any of these calls signify the beginning of the awakening of the self, leading to personal transformation. A call is a release from some restrictive circumstance and the letting go of what we think we need to hold on to. It is a time of seeking out or encountering the unknown, which can create an atmosphere of irresistible fascination or curiosity. The call also refers to being called to a vocation in a spiritual sense.

A variation to this opening motif is when we are not ready to begin something new in our life. The motif would then be *Refusal of the Call*. This is when some kind of pressure, commitment, status quo, or vested interest keeps us where we are. We may even hope that the status quo remains, as in a faltering marriage. This motif means that we don't want to give up what we have for something we don't know. Sometimes we may need to be rescued from our complacency. We could also accept the call, step back, reconsider, and decide to refuse it again. Our mythic quest may be foreclosed if we are too attached to our present status.

Next is the motif of *Assistance*. After we enter the archetypal realm that can be anything new to us, we soon recognize that we are never alone. We always seem to encounter a protective figure, someone that is in the right place at the right time, to help us through an impasse. We know now we are under the protective hand of destiny.

In traditional literature, this aid usually comes in the form of a supernatural helper, a power animal, or a wise elder. In all cases, the assistance brings with it the sensation and assurance that we are being inwardly guided. A feeling of being carried along toward some as-yet unknown end, which nothing or no one can prevent, may also become evident.

Today's versions of this aid may come from close friends, counselors or therapists, mentors, doctors or healers, teachers, a book we read, or even from the forces of the universe that seem to be working with us. Receiving this assistance is the sign we get when we are following our bliss. It is believing in "a Power greater than ourselves" (Step 2). On an inner level, this is when we are working in harmony with the forces of our unconscious. The mystics, as well as all the world's religions, call this "grace."

Another motif of this part is *The Initial Challenge*. Even though we are being guided, all is not clear sailing. The balance begins to shift again, and things get a little rough. We pass deeper into new territory (external or internal), and—in a classic sense—formidable powers pop up. We may get a warning of an impending danger as we look beyond where we are and into the darkness of what might lie ahead for us. Yet this is but the first obstacle we face in testing our courage and commitment to what we have begun. Attainment of our goal is not going to come easy.

Contemporary versions of this motif, of crossing the first threshold, include any experience that gives us a new level of challenges to deal with, such as beginning graduate work, raising children for the first time, a promotion, more responsibilities, doing something new, struggles in a marriage, and fears of what lies ahead. This motif means we need to summon our courage and advance toward the danger anyway. This is our first test of faith that allows us "to turn our will and our lives over to the care of God as we understand Him" (Step 3). As we make the effort toward the obstacles in our path, we discover that the barriers seem to fade away and let us pass beyond them.

The final motif of this first phase is that of *Retreat*. There comes a time when we need to step back, reconsider things, take care of ourselves, and make our own final preparations for the next threshold. It can be a conscious or unconscious withdrawal, but it is a time to reassess where we are and where we may be going and to do the serious work of looking inward, which ultimately aids our renewal.

The classic example of this motif is Jonah entering the belly of the whale. He didn't plan his withdrawal this way, but it was just what he needed. He left the commonplace world behind, was actually cut off from it, and sacrificed something of himself in the process. In withdrawing, we symbolically shed the old, no-longer useful or meaningful ways, and begin to seriously turn inward to prepare for self-renewal. Modern-day versions of this might include entering therapy, living alone, being laid up with an illness, shutting ourselves off from others, adjusting to being a new parent, or just going on a planned retreat. This would also be the time during which we make a "searching and fearless moral inventory of ourselves" (Step 4).

The following exercise is meant to help you recall some of your own experiences that parallel the above motifs. First, choose a block of time when you won't be disturbed, and find a place for quiet reflection where you can think back to some of your own key experiences.

When you are ready and comfortable, let your mind come to rest and meditate on these two thoughts for a few moments: Letting go is necessary for reaching out. Retreat is preparation for emergence.

Now, follow your own path backward to those times in your life when something really changed for you. Think about each one as you come to it. Maybe one of these experiences sticks out the most. Maybe they are all equally important in your mind now.

Ask yourself these questions about those times in your life: Which new phase of my life seems to have had the deepest, longest lasting effect on my life? What did I leave behind? Did I know where I was headed?

Did I ever have the experience of being helped by someone or something or being inwardly guided when I most needed it? Who or what was it that was guiding me?

Have I ever felt like I had to summon all my courage to overcome a new or dangerous predicament? What was it that was in my way at the time, that I had to overcome? Did the danger seem to fade away as I faced it?

Was there ever a time when I just had to stop everything and turned inward? Did it feel like I was cut off from the rest of the world?

Stay with these thoughts for as long as you need to. The experiences you have come up with are probably connected to each other as a series of events. Try to identify the common thread that links them. When you are ready, transfer your thoughts to the worksheet in Exhibit 5.2, filling in your personal experiences on the lines across from the motifs that they parallel.

### Part 1—Beginning

With this exercise, you will develop your own experiences from the separation phase into the first part of the story that will become your personal myth. The beginning of your mythic adventure focuses on the initiating event that signaled a new phase of your life and led you into some new and unknown realms.

Think about the form and style that would best fit your experience. Feel free to be as creative, imaginative, and open as you can in expressing these experiences as a story. You will want to write your personal myth in a style or genre that is most comfortable to you; it could be realistic, allegorical, impressionistic, or some combination thereof. Remember that what you are telling is your inner truth, that part of your life that most connects with the lives of others.

Now take your rough notes from the previous exercise, your personal motifs (your own life events and experiences) and what they mean to you, and turn them into a flowing narrative that includes all of your experiences paralleling the first phase of the mythic pattern.

When you have your first draft completed, take some more time to look it over, being sure that you have captured the essence of that experience as clearly as possible, before going on to Phase Two of your personal myth.

Exhibit 5.2
Personal Mythmaking Worksheet: Separation Motifs

| *Archetypal Experiences & What They Mean* | *Personal Experiences & What They Mean* |
|---|---|
| **THE CALL TO ADVENTURE** (setting off on a quest) leaving home, moving, divorce, getting married, becoming pregnant, a new career, a serious illness, a new way of seeing things <u>MEANING:</u> a familiar pattern is broken, awakening of the inner self, encountering the unknown, beginning of a transformation | |
| **ASSISTANCE** (supernatural aid) help from a friend, a therapist, a lawyer, a mentor, a teacher, a doctor, a book, or the universe <u>MEANING:</u> a protective power appears, we are never alone, feeling inwardly guided | |
| **THE INITIAL CHALLENGE** (crossing the first threshold) new struggles, fears, arise <u>MEANING:</u> test of courage, danger fades as we advance | |
| **RETREAT** (belly of the whale) entering therapy, living alone, laid up with an illness <u>MEANING:</u> withdrawal, reassessment, taking care of ourselves, turning inward | |

## PHASE TWO: INITIATION

This is where things get the roughest. After retreat, our time in the belly of the whale, we are partially renewed or at least revived and strengthened enough to be better prepared for the difficulties we are about to encounter.

The initiation phase signals an intense period of *Greater Challenges*. Here, we meet with various tests and difficult tasks, all in succession. In order to continue and progress onward in the process we have started, we need somehow to overcome these even greater obstacles that appear before us.[8]

In classic mythology, all sorts of trials and ordeals, conquests, and symbolic figures arise to complicate the external landscape traversed by the hero: dragons, warriors, wicked witches, and even the depths of the under-world.

In our modern world, however, our trials are just as often inner struggles where we are forced to face all that lies within us and to come to know the internal landscape of our psyche more than we had before. This is the heart of the transformation process. If there is no muddle, there can be no resolution. Examples of this motif today might include having to submerge or sacrifice our true aspirations, suffering life-threatening illness, experiences of abuse (or even self-abuse), thoughts of dying or attempts at suicide, struggling over the conflict between personal beliefs and personal behavior, severe financial burdens, being expected to accomplish something without having the means to do it, not being able to find a job, doing difficult work in therapy, or any other personal struggle that eventually leads to our purification and being able to embrace all aspects of ourselves.

The quality of *acceptance* is crucial to the process. We not only have to understand what lies within us, but we have to be able to accept it all. This may be the point at which, in the twelve-step programs, we "admit to God, to ourselves, and to another human being, the exact nature of our wrongs" (Step 5). This helps us realize and utilize our hidden capabilities and brings us much closer to our own rebirth.

Another motif of this phase is *Further Assistance*. Soon after we have experienced the most difficult time of the process, we may get an early, preliminary glimpse of what we have sought in our deepest wishes. It may be but a sign of what is yet to come, because it is also usually only a temporary glimpse.

In classic mythology, this is the meeting with the goddess. She represents everything that has ever been sought, all in one perfect form. She also represents all that can be known.

In contemporary form, examples of this motif might be support from others just when it is needed, digging deeper into our creative resources, the renewal of a relationship, new realizations of what we do have, or, on an inner level, the male meeting his feminine side, the female encountering her masculine side, or either glimpsing their spirit nature.

Primarily, this signals an expansion of consciousness, with a picture of wholeness, in which a brief meeting with our future self is temporarily glanced upon. It comes to us as a promise of what we might find after we are fully renewed.

Usually following this is the motif of *Temptation*. To make sure we are deserving of, and ready for, what could lie ahead, we may encounter temptations of many forms. They often hit us at our weakest point, as something we may have been struggling with for a long time. A temptation directed at a weakness may keep coming back until we have mastered it.

In the classic hero myth, it is most often the woman who is the temptress. Her irresistible beauty is the final test of the hero. If he succumbs, an innocent delight may become an agony to the spirit. For a woman, man is often the tempter. At this point in the journey of transformation it is the purity of soul that is uppermost in guiding our every move.

In our contemporary world, we could be tempted by an affair, unethical conduct at work, substance abuse, or any number of the dysfunctional compulsions and characteristics we are prone to these days. If we are well grounded in the spiritual awakening that is happening to us at this point, the temptation may make us "ready to have God remove all these defects of character," "our shortcomings," and to help us make "direct amends" to the people we have harmed (Steps 6 through 10 of the twelve steps).

Another contemporary form of this motif is our tendency to want instant gratification. When we become aware of what we see as a need, that need seems to grow and grow in our mind, getting all out of proportion. If we are thirsty, our thirst continues to grow and grow. All we want is something to satisfy our thirst. Our mind focuses on what it will be like to quench our thirst; we may even envision a huge waterfall that we can drink from. We want it all right now. Temptations do this to us. But temptations come to us to help us put things in their proper perspective and to learn, perhaps over and over again, that life, especially its bounties, come a little at a time, usually a drop at a time. Understanding temptations means giving up the idea of the waterfall and being content with one drop at a time.

Whatever the temptation, this is when our ideals and values need to be made as clear as possible. This is when we become the most serious about examining our own lives and on an ongoing basis. Temptations can reappear at any time, and the purpose of this motif is to give us a greater depth of self-knowledge to be able to handle any and all temptations.

The final motif in this phase, after overcoming our temptations, is *Renewal and Rebirth*. In classic mythology, this motif begins with an atonement, most often a reconciliation with the father, so that there is no longer an estrangement impeding our progress toward rebirth. This could also mean becoming atoned with God through conscious and regular prayer and meditation and by a strong desire to live His will (Step 11). The secret here is that grace is hidden within that which makes us fearful.

This signifies letting go of the selfish ego and actually experiencing an initiatory, or symbolic, death. In reestablishing contact with that which we become one with, we ensure a strong foundation upon which threats lose their power and fears gradually vanish.

This allows for the full release of our potential, and perhaps for the first time we take on the new role of guide in a very important situation. This enables us to understand and experience "grace" in a new and deeper way, and also to feel a strong sense of accomplishment and peacefulness.

In both a mythic and modern sense, we are reborn as more than we were. Today, this can take the form of deep insights and progress in therapy, a greater degree of self-awareness than ever before, taking control of our life, an "ah-ha" or peak experience, new achievements or accomplishments, seeing things around us for the first time, or really knowing a peacefulness and calmness in our lives that we hadn't before. We need to remember here that at our moment of great triumph, we are also at our most vulnerable.

We have the greater responsibility now of knowing our androgynous nature better, that our personal prejudices can be broken free of, and of feeling a compassion for all life. We want to be able to see all around us that which we feel within us. In looking back, it seems not only that our vision is greater than our speech but also that this has been a transformation that happened to us, rather than one we brought about on our own.

Set aside some time now in your quiet place, where you can go back in time to identify the motifs that fit your experience of the initiation phase of the pattern. When you are ready, meditate on this thought for a few moments: *Out of crisis comes opportunity.*

Now, go back in your life to those times when things were the most difficult for you. Think about these times, and ask yourself the following questions: When I was going through these trials, what difficulties was I having, what ordeals did I have to overcome? Did I discover any hidden capacities when I faced these ordeals? Did I find myself feeling cleansed or purified during this process?

Was there anyone or anything during this time that gave me a clearer sense of what was to come? What was this vision of the future? Did someone or something seem to distract me from my goal? How did I handle this situation?

What has been my greatest sense of accomplishment or experience of renewal? Did that bring with it a new role, greater responsibility, or inner peace? Did that include restoring a relationship with someone close to me? Did I feel as though my inner potential was within reach? What ideals, values, goals, or gifts did this experience give me?

After you have thought about these questions adequately, you are ready to transfer what you have come up with to the worksheet in Exhibit 5.3.

Exhibit 5.3
Personal Mythmaking Worksheet: Initiation Motifs

| *Archetypal Experiences* *& What They Mean* | *Personal Experiences* *& What They Mean* |
| --- | --- |
| **GREATER CHALLENGES** (road of trials) inner struggles, conflicts, sacrificing aspirations, suffering with an illness, experiences of abuse, lack of resources    MEANING: discovering hidden ability, purification of the self, need to be tempered, | _____ _____ _____ _____ _____ |
| **FURTHER ASSISTANCE** (meeting with the goddess) support from others, using inner resources, a glimpse of the future    MEANING: a glimpse of wholeness, expansion of consiousness, encountering our shadow side | _____ _____ _____ _____ _____ |
| **TEMPTATION** (woman as temptress) having an affair, unethical conduct, substance abuse, compulsions, instant gratification    MEANING: innocence transcended, personal standards tested, ideals and values are set | _____ _____ _____ _____ _____ |
| **RENEWAL AND REBIRTH** (atonement, apotheosis, boon) taking control of your life, peak experience, inner peace, insight and change in therapy    MEANING: old self dies, mysteries become clear, potential released, gift to be given back | _____ _____ _____ _____ _____ |

### Part 2—Muddle

This exercise helps you develop your personal motifs from the initiation phase into the middle portion of your personal myth. This will most likely be a continuation of part 1 of your personal myth, although it could pick things up at a later point in your life, too. You will probably see a common web of meaning linking the events of this phase to the events of the first part.

This middle part of your personal myth reveals the inherent promise of your life, in which your life takes on a new and more purposeful direction. In this portion, you resolve personal conflicts and experience an important personal triumph, through an expansion of consciousness.

Now, continuing on in the style you used in the first part, focus on the difficulties, ordeals, victories, and renewal you just outlined on the worksheet, and turn these personal motifs (your life experiences, and what they mean to you), into a clear, flowing story, being sure to express yourself with as much feeling as you possibly can.

After completing your first draft, give yourself enough time to really take in all the implications of this major change in your life before going on to Phase Three.


### PHASE THREE: RETURN

After the experience of rebirth and the sensation of peacefulness, we encounter a new kind of test. That is the challenge of what to do next. What do we do with what we have been given? How do we even attempt to pass this new understanding on to anyone else? Do we even want to, if we could? Would anyone come close to understanding if we tried to tell them what it meant to us and how it has changed us? Would anyone even listen?

There may be the temptation to remain in isolation and enjoy our boon alone, or there may be circumstances preventing us from doing anything. Even the great saviors, like Buddha, doubted whether they could communicate to others the experience of their enlightenment.

Thus, this phase begins with the motif of *Responsibility Accepted or Refused*. We can either deny the world and give our own needs priority over those of others, be prevented from returning due to some external factors, or experience full support in returning with the elixir. This motif often includes all three possibilities in sequence.[9]

In classic mythology, this motif translates as a refusal to return with what we have been given, or responsibility shrugged; magic flight, or obstacles being thrown in our way; and receiving assistance to return with our boon. Today, we could express this motif as feeling more responsible to ourselves or family than to others, feeling as though the timing is not quite right for giving to others, feeling overwhelmed or insecure, worrying about being accepted, as well as getting support from those closest to us, and feeling wanted or welcome by others.

The fulfillment of this motif is to return with something to show for where we have been and what we have been doing all this time. It doesn't have to be much. It just has to be what we have learned from our experience of transformation, of discovering who we really are in the depths of our being. The successful return is always an illustration of what is humanly possible.

After deciding it is all important to give back what we have been given, in some form appropriate to our means, the challenge is surviving the impact of the world. This means returning to the common-day world after a fabulous adventure without feeling let down, even if what we bring back is misunderstood, disregarded, or trivialized. The blow of the harsh realities of the world may be too much for us, or we can learn to accept the inevitable disbelief and criticism we get in life. It may seem as though we are living in two separate worlds, the divine (from where we received our boon) and the human.

So this motif presents yet another test for us. Survival at this point depends upon the realization that the two worlds are but different parts of the same whole, though they appear as night and day. Others may seem oblivious to what we have found, but we have to learn to live our own lives and give to others at the same time. Maintaining a balance between our inner needs and our outer responsibility may be one of our greatest challenges. Detachment is again a key to living in the world after we have had the experience of transformation.

Our task at this point in the process is to figure out the most appropriate means for us to pass on our particular gift to others. It may be through our work, another role in life, or some creative expression. But this is going to be made more difficult because those we want to most reach may have a very different experience than we do, and we must somehow make ours as clear and understandable as we can for them.

We are now very close to a new beginning, and we need to understand the importance of surrender once again as we did at the beginning of the process. We have become more familiar with the feeling of being guided by invisible hands. We have learned to trust in our own destiny as well as to make our own efforts. It helps at this point to be grateful for what we have been given and for what we have experienced. We are not perfect yet, and never will be, but if we can just let go of our personal limitations, characteristics, idiosyncrasies, and even our hopes to some degree, they may let go of us. When we are able to give these up, we may even find that something we like better will take their place. We have a much better chance at this if we know that grace continually surrounds us.

The whole meaning of personal mythmaking is to explore the hidden realms of what has happened in our lives, incorporate all of it into our consciousness, and live accordingly. This will help us survive the impact of the world and its disappointments and maintain self-assurance in the face of it all.

Last is the motif of *Living Consciously*. To complete the mythic pattern, we not only have to return some of what we have received, we have to remember that we are always in the process of becoming. One way of looking at this is that we are always striving to get our will in harmony with the universal will. This is also the final step of the twelve-step programs and means that "we tried to carry this message" to others and "to practice these principles in all our affairs."

Living this motif means being always active, doing whatever our role in life calls for, and being content and pleased with our lot. We can accept our shortcomings along with our successes and feel responsible only for our own actions. We enjoy our life, and feel that we are where we need to be, contributing something of benefit to others, without expecting anything in return.

This is the true meaning of the provider becoming the nurturer, and the seeker becoming the sage. We give without expectation, knowing that this whole pattern may often repeat itself, that we may have many "calls," many "initiations," and many "returns," and that with each one we will continue to grow spiritually and help others do the same. We also come to realize that the story of the whole experience gradually becomes more important than the facts contained within it.

Take some time now, in your quiet place, where you can look back to a special time in your life. Meditate for a few moments, on this thought: *What we have been given is ours to give back.*

Now, think back to those times in your life when you felt as though you had something to give others and were able to do so. Recall as much as you can about these times, and ask yourself the following questions: Were you ever reluctant, afraid, or unable to share an exhilarating experience with another? Did it ever seem like you had something important to say but were prevented from communicating this? Were you ever assisted in helping someone in a way that you didn't quite understand at the time? Did you ever try to share something of real importance to you but have it misunderstood or disregarded? How did you handle this disappointment? Has offering someone something of importance to you ever helped maintain your self-assurance or commitment? Have you been able to accept your limitations along with your achievements?

What is the one vision, dream, or goal that you live for? Have you ever felt that your life is in harmony with some higher order? What is the real meaning of the feelings you have just recalled? Transfer your thoughts from this exercise to the worksheet in Exhibit 5.4.

Exhibit 5.4
Personal Mythmaking Worksheet: Return Motifs

| *Archetypal Experiences & What They Mean* | *Personal Experiences & What They Mean* |
|---|---|
| **RESPONSIBILITY ACCEPTED OR REFUSED** (Magic flight) timing not right, obstacles prevent return | _____ _____ |
|     MEANING:   worried about acceptance,   feeling insecure | _____ |
| (Rescue) getting support, welcomed by others | _____ _____ |
|     MEANING:   our return is supported | _____ |
| (Crossing the return threshold) surviving the impact, being understood, our gift is received, harsh realities are handled, we accept what comes our way | _____ _____ _____ |
|     MEANING: we have a desire to share our gift with others, the return is a test of our commitment, we are grateful for our gift, self-assurance is maintained | _____ _____ _____ |
| **LIVING CONSCIOUSLY** (Master of two worlds, Freedom to live) doing what our roles call for, carrying the message, successes and failures , joys and sorrows are accepted, contentment with our role and place in life | _____ _____ _____ _____ |
|     MEANING: our gift is given proper expression, we are always becoming, we are where we need to be, our individual will and the universal will are in harmony, we have realized our goals, and are ready for new challenges | _____ _____ _____ _____ _____ |

### Part 3—Bringing Back the Boon

This exercise focuses on the events representing your return to the common-day world as a new person. You may have felt like you didn't want to return, weren't ready to return, or were inadequate to even try to share what you had been given. Or you may have felt that no one would understand what you had to give anyway. Or, with support from somewhere or a desire to return, you may have willingly brought your boon back to benefit others.

This conclusion of your personal myth reveals the promise fulfilled of your life, when you are able to understand your role in and contribution to the world. Though this may be consciously understood now, it may involve a long, frustrating process of further growth, adaptation, and effort to actually achieve what you know is within the realm of possibility, but you have the assurance now that it is all worth the effort.

Take the time to focus your thoughts, keeping in mind that this part of your story represents primarily a personal victory. Now, continuing in the style of your first two parts, develop your personal motifs from the return phase, and what they mean to you, into story form. This will become the conclusion of your personal myth: a complete, whole story, with a beginning, middle, and end.


After you have completed this third part of your personal myth, you may want to reflect on what the three parts mean to you as a whole.

Having told the core of our life story as a personal myth, we can see more clearly now that our psychological growth follows a path parallel to that of the mythic pattern. Both are a process that focus on personal transformation. This path not only changes us, making us more than we were, it also inspires us in new directions. Traveling this path of personal transformation makes us value our own life and that of others, more. We want to share more of our own life and our life story with others, and help others express more of theirs in some way.

We also come to see that life has a structure, or pattern, to it, which we live out. The more familiar we are with the basic cycle in our lives of crisis and victory, the more comfortable we will be with our lives as a whole and the more accepting we will become with everything that does happen in our lives.

At the same time, we understand that it is this very pattern that gives us the freedom to pursue the things we want to in the way that feels best to us and also gives us the means by which we become the most of what we are capable of becoming. We become more of who we really are by knowing that we have lived out this ageless pattern in our own lives and that it has taken us through an experience of transformation. There is great value for us in knowing the mythic motifs that the gods and goddesses have lived out in their lives, because they tell us much about basic human experiences and even more about what is possible for us.

If we discover our own way, consciously, through this process, we come to know what Campbell called its ultimate aim, "neither release nor ecstasy for oneself, but the wisdom and the power to serve others."[10] This is the essential message, the common truth, that the inner life of humanity has expressed forever.

To go through the process of personal transformation, to really live truly mythically, is to come out the other side as a "real," "complete" person in the sense that we have seen the best and worst of what life has to offer anyone. We emerge with qualities that make us fully human.

We have had to leave something very familiar and comfortable behind; we have made sacrifices. We have been helped when we thought there was no hope in sight for us. We have met and overcome obstacles that were personally threatening to us. We have been alone, cut off from others and the world, and didn't know when we would ever be with others again.

We were tested with trials and ordeals that pushed us to our limits. We were wounded, but we endured. We saw a glimpse of how wonderful things could be for us, and we yearned for this joy. We were tested some more, this time for our integrity and the standard that we could uphold. We were able to resolve old hurts or reconcile old differences. We learned that grace often comes from where we least expect it. We were able to let go of the old, unwanted parts of our self, to let them die. We felt renewed, reborn, more than we ever had been. We felt more whole, more complete, than we ever had. We felt free of what had been restricting us, and we felt much more compassion for others. We understood that we are vulnerable, even at our moment of greatest strength. We knew that we had something to give to others, but that our vision was greater than our speech.

We were tested once again, to see if we were really committed to what we had discovered about ourselves and our world. We were clear about our priorities, and tried to give back some of what we had been given, even though we knew it might be misunderstood, disregarded, or even trivialized. We maintained our newfound sensitivity to others, remembering that we could only do so much, anyway. Our empathy for others grew the more we gave of ourselves. We learned to accept our limitations along with our successes, maintaining our assurance in the face of whatever comes. And we became content with our lot in life, trying to live interdependently and in harmony with the world of which we are an important part.

We now know the greatest story in the world and have lived to tell our own version of it!

## NOTES

1. Jung, *Memories, dreams, reflections*, p. 3.

2. Estes, *Women who run with the wolves*, pp. 30, 270–71.

3. *Jung, Memories, dreams, reflections*, p. 3.

4. Eliade, *Rites and symbols of initiation*.

5. Murdock, *The heroine's journey*, p. 5.

6. Campbell, *The hero with a thousand faces*, p. 30.

7. For more details on the Separation phase, read Campbell, *The hero with a thousand faces*, pp. 49–95.

8. For more details on the Initiation phase, read Campbell, pp. 97–192.

9. For more details on the Return phase, read Campbell, pp. 193–244.

10. Campbell, *Myths to live by*, p. 227.

# 6

## *Merging Your Personal Myth With the Collective Myth*

Where we had thought to travel outward, we shall come to the center of our own existence; where we had thought to be alone, we shall be with all the world.[1]

Our personal myth highlights the strong threads that make up our own life experience and at the same time reveals the common threads that we share with all of humanity. By giving voice to our story, we find that we tell a familiar story. The part is a reflection of the whole. The whole is greater than its parts, yet the two together tell one story.

Personal images that emerge through remembrance of things past often reach out to us from the center of human experience. Such images speak to us in an exhilarating, universal language, assuring us that our own images are greater than ourselves. What is at the center of our own existence not only connects us to all the world, but is also the most profound and therefore the most difficult to explain. Our personal story, at its essence, is the human story.

Each of us has the same basic blueprint within us, yet each of us lives it out in our unique way. The blueprint comes from the collective, and when we recognize similarities in our experiences, we become aware of the blueprint of life that we all share. The collective guides the personal, and the personal serves the collective. The fundamental goal of the hero/ine myth is to attain the boon and share it with others.

The classic myths, the personal myths we live, and the stories we tell about ourselves, all reflect the sacred pattern of life. This pattern has guided history and human progress forever. That pattern, once more, is *beginning, muddle, resolution,* or *birth, death, rebirth.* In its simplest form, it is *crisis followed by victory,* over and over again.

When a living myth breaks down, dies, or is no longer effective, we go through a period of chaos, confusion, alienation, meaninglessness, and spiritual loneliness. This is the result of the values and truths breaking down that hold society together. Yet it is these same values and truths that speak to us the loudest in our own lives when we are searching for meaning and truth. When we need these guiding principles the most, they come into our lives. They are essential to the renewal of society and our own personal lives.

If it feels like our world is in a time of chaos and meaninglessness, we are in the *crisis* phase of the pattern; it could also be that the renewal phase is already underway. Both phases can happen simultaneously, without our being aware of it. Death, or disintegration of a living myth, is followed by the rebirth of the same timeless truth, adapted to a newer time. And when a potent, living myth begins to emerge, to be reborn, it elicits the passionate response of all who are aware of it. It becomes a rallying force to live by.

Historians are well aware of this pattern. It has repeated itself throughout time. The rise and fall of civilizations mirror this cyclical pattern, as does economy. Fifty years ago, Japan was a devastated nation, today it is a world leader. As Mircea Eliade says, "In each period of peace, history renews itself and, consequently, a new world begins."[2] Economic cycles are renewed, too, as it was for the United States after the depression.

Not only does this pattern make everything possible for us, it also means that a great deal depends upon us. We could stay in a period of chaos forever, if we let ourselves. Or we could each collaborate, to the extent of our capacity, in the renewal of the guiding myth. In fact, it is the carrying out of our individual responsibility to the whole that ensures its renewal.

Our awareness of this responsibility brings with it the burden of giving back to others something of what we have been given. This awareness "does not shut one out from the world, but gathers the world to oneself,"[3] as Jung said. Understanding this tells us that our own experience is greater than ourselves, but it also humbles us. With this realization, we may feel, as Jung has said, that "we are no longer individuals, but the race," that "the voice of all mankind resounds in us."[4]

One of the primary functions of myth is to provide us with a view of the world that parallels our own experience and clarifies the meaning of our existence in the world. What our personal myth does, I think, is reflect what is collectively possible for the time in which we live.

## THE GUIDING MYTH OF OUR TIME

What is the message we would want to bring back with us from our journey to the depths of our soul to share with everyone else? What are the archetypes guiding the evolution of our collective mythology? Do these add up to the new myth of our time? In discussing the guiding truths of our time, the archetypes of this new mythology, and how our personal myths fit with that, I can only offer some of my own experience, tell you what some other people have found from their experience, and ask some questions that may help you determine how the guiding myth fits with your life.

We have lived a unique experience in this century. Over and over again, we have come to the crossroads of history. Once more, as a new century beckons, we approach another critical crossroads affecting our collective survival.

Has the "Great Vision" of Black Elk become a rallying cry for today? We now have a better understanding of what he was talking about when he said, "While I stood there I saw more than I can tell and I understood more than I saw; for I was seeing in a sacred manner the shapes of all things in the spirit, and the shape of all shapes as they must live together like one being. And I saw that the sacred hoop of my people was one of many hoops that made one circle, wide as daylight and as starlight, and in the center grew one mighty flowering tree to shelter all the children of one mother and one father. And I saw that it was holy."[5]

Has our reality caught up with his vision? An event that made this understanding possible for us was our ability to leave our own world behind for a moment and look at it from a totally new perspective. It was only from the moon that we were able to put down our maps and see that there really aren't any boundaries between us. Our view of our world from the moon confirmed what the great visionaries and prophets of earlier times had told us from their journey to their depths.

The 1969 moon walk was enthusiastically hailed by many as a great adventure of the ages. Did this one event, with its mass media coverage, speed up our conscious awareness of our common destiny? Did that event, that vivid image of our planet with no boundaries between us, signal the beginning of a global transformation?

Following the moon walk a series of events took place in my own life that did signal the beginning of a personal transformation that I had written about as my personal myth, *Seasons of the Soul*, and relate in chapters 1 and 3.

Though I am an only child, my experiences, which included being welcomed into stranger's homes as if I were part of their family, showed me that we are all part of a world community. It took some time however for my intellect to catch up with my experience.

I struggled to maintain this perspective of unity and wholeness while carrying out my daily life. The difficulty was in letting that feeling guide my every thought and action—not an easy thing to do. My challenge was to be able to live as the master of the two worlds I was moving back and forth between: the world of my vision where everything was one, and the world of daily life where everything was separate and even confusing at times. When I realized that the two worlds are really one and the same, that the separation was only in my mind, this made it a little easier.

Even though my experience was so strong and vivid that it wouldn't go away, I still needed further validation for my experience. After I returned home from Norway, I wrote the first draft of my personal myth that I had just lived. But I still wanted to know how my experience, and newly acquired world view, fit with what else was out there. I read as much about mythology and comparative religion as I could find. I became fascinated with the question Jung had asked in his autobiography: In what myth do we live today?[6] I wanted to know what underlying truth is guiding our lives at this time in our history. If it is not what once guided us, what is it?

I felt that the only living myth that could guide us all today would be one that would strike a chord of resonance within us when experienced, felt, or even thought about. What deep truth of the human spirit calls out to us the loudest today? What speaks most strongly to our soul, inspiring us in divine directions? Whatever it is, this is what gives voice to our innermost dreams.

When it comes to finding a new mythology, a new guiding truth, that can fill the void around us—that can be a myth, a truth, we can live with—the first place to turn is our own story, our own truth, our own spirituality, our own search for meaning. We must go back into our own experience to find our own inner certainties. This means, each in our own way, finding the answers to the really important questions: "What am I certain about?" "What have I experienced?" "What is my story?" Our own autobiographical truth has a great deal to teach us about our relationship with others and the world we live in.

What seems evident in our time is that there are two forces in operation at the same time, the old and the new, the dying myth and the emerging myth. Is the separateness of the old myth still practical today? Or, as we move closer to a global economy, indeed, a global village, is the emerging myth of harmony and inclusiveness practical and truthful for today?

I recently pulled out my copy of *Creative Mythology* that Joseph Campbell gave me on a March 2, 1973 visit to his home, which he had signed with his "best wishes." In the beginning of the book he offers his reflections on having completed the four-volume *Masks of God*:

> I find that its main result for me has been its confirmation of a thought I have long and faithfully entertained: of the unity of the race of man, not only in its biology but also in its spiritual history, which has everywhere unfolded in the manner of a single symphony, . . . irresistibly advancing to some kind of mighty climax, out of which the next great movement will emerge. And I can see no reason why anyone should suppose that in the future the same

motifs already heard will not be sounding still—in new relationships indeed, but ever the same motifs.[7]

If "the unity of the race of man" is the primary archetype of the myth of our time, what are the supporting archetypes that we will need to be able to recognize in "new relationships"? Such secondary archetypes would have to be those that promote unity.

I was intrigued with what psychologist Rollo May had to say about this in a filmed interview I saw as part of my counseling program in 1980. In speaking about the role of cultural myths in our lives, and about the time in which we now live, he made the point very clearly that we live in a time of a crisis of the spirit, a crisis of personal and collective truth, because the guiding symbols of myth have broken down.[8]

What are we to do in this situation? Rollo May's answer is that we had best live with the myths of the future, with what is going to be the spiritual center of our world to come. Each one of us must try to find the myths and symbols that we genuinely believe the future will be founded upon. Our responsibility, individually to ourselves and to society, is to find the myths and symbols we believe will become most important in the future. May then listed what he considered to be the guiding symbols and archetypes of the new mythology: the symbol of one world, the symbol of interacialism, women's liberation, and an economic system that values the worker.

These symbols, which might make up the guiding myth of our time, made sense to me because they matched my own experience. I had become very familiar with the principle of one world from my own travels. My own experience of seeing that we are all one human family, and that we all share in the responsibility of caring for our planet Earth, was then confirmed in my own study, readings, and realizations, including my investigation of the Baha'i Faith, where these same symbols are described as the principles of a new world order leading to unity and lasting peace.[9]

In his latest book, *The Cry for Myth*, Rollo May explores the emerging archetype of the "liberation of women" further. Civilization will never be complete, he says, as long as half of the people in it are considered inferior. Our modern culture lacks myths and rituals giving significance to a woman's life separate from what she has in relation to a man. Liberation, for women and for men, means both are free to be what they inherently are and to pursue the opportunities they desire.[10]

These symbols could well be the key to our future. Recognizing our oneness, curing the disease of racism, establishing a gender equality that works, and eliminating the economic extremes in the world could help a great deal to bring about the collective future we would want for our children's children, a future in which harmony, justice, and balance are the bywords.

When we have found those guiding symbols and archetypes that we really feel will lead us into the future we want, then our responsibility is to live our lives based on them. These guiding principles have been mirrors for me to gaze upon in determining my own values, my own identity, and ultimately my own personal myth. They also fit the archetypal pattern we have been looking at. Each symbol presents a conflict, whose resolution will lead to renewal, on both the personal and collective levels.

Yet, another important "emerging" principle is our own determined search for personal truth. We will always be thwarted in our effort to understand who we are at our core, and what our own beliefs are, if we do not seriously try to distinguish false from true for ourselves. We each have to seek our own truth, as is done in the vision quest. This then becomes the source of guidance for the rest of our lives.

What is our own vision of the future? Is liberation of us all a prerequisite for unity? Is this what will help bring about a more equitable balance between the feminine and masculine influences in society? The myth that will ensure our collective survival, May says, is "the myth of human kind." Though this new myth has not yet changed us all, through it we may achieve a new international morality. This is "a myth of a new age," according to May, that "gives us images that come alive." Is this the voice of a thousand souls speaking, echoing what we all want to hear?

Robert Johnson suggests that "the Great Quest" is no longer that of the conquering (masculine) hero, who defends his territory, his principles, his woman, his rights, but that of the embracing hero, who finds the right place for each relationship in life, who nurtures and protects and comforts so that growth can take place, not in a field of illusions, but in a field of love and wholeness.[11] Is our heroic task "to learn to love—if our planet and our civilization are to survive much beyond our present era?"

Are we on the threshold of a completely new level of evolution, as different from consciousness as consciousness is from life, as life is from matter? Are we, as Peter Russell has said, witnessing the emergence of a "global brain"?[12]

If the collective myth in which we are living today is founded upon planetary transformation, leading us away from ego-centeredness and to a unified field of shared awareness, what will each of our life stories, our personal myths, look like in order for this dramatic change to actually take place?

These are the questions. The answers are within you, in your own experience, within the truth that makes up your story. To know the questions is to be on a quest. To be on a quest is to be open, to be ready. Our own questions help us make sense of our own experience. What follows is an exercise to explore a bit more in depth how your personal myth relates to what may be the myth of our time, and how you may carry out your role in this grand transformation.

## MASTER OF TWO WORLDS

Our personal myth carries a dual role, that of serving ourselves and serving others in some way, too. This exercise is designed to help you discover how you can accomplish both simultaneously. Your personal myth, especially the return portion, probably made it clear to you that you have some role, however large or small, in the grand scheme of things. You probably understand now, if you hadn't before, that you have something to offer others.

Think a bit more about your role in your family, community, and the larger context of the world. What is the most important issue or goal in your life that in some way also impacts on the lives of others? What is the one value or belief you want to live your life for?

How does your personal myth allow you to be master of both your own personal life and also contribute in some way to the collective life of us all? How will you carry out your role in both worlds, the human and the divine, and pass back and forth between them, understanding that they are but two aspects of the same whole?

What is your view of the guiding myth the world needs? What is your "vision" of the collective future of humanity? What role do you want to play in this vision? In what ways does your experience, the essence of your personal truth, reflect what you see unfolding in the world around you, and how will your life be a contribution to this unfolding? In other words, what's the "big picture," and how do you fit in? What resources do you feel are at your disposal to assist you in carrying this out?

Meditate on these questions for a while. As thoughts come to your mind, write them down in note form first. After you have had time to reflect on these thoughts, turn your notes into a flowing narrative that expresses how your life fits into the whole, as you see it.

Here is the voice of a nurse, having reflected upon these questions:

My personal myth destined me to deal with addiction. Born into a family of alcoholics, gamblers, and co-addicts, I lived at home for twenty years. After leaving home, my life continued to take me back to the source, the world of addiction, where I lived for another fifteen years. Those were painful years, but necessary for the spiritual transformation that took place when I was forced to face my demons two-and-a-half-years ago. The turning point for me was experiencing the miracle that occurs when people come together to share the stories of their suffering, their descent, and their return to life. I felt the power of love and hope, the healing, that had transformed those lives to a state of quiet serenity. I wanted what they had. I made a personal vow to life, a vow to create a new way of being. A choice for recovery.

My greatest personal challenge is my commitment to spiritual growth and development. I am concerned with the profound questions of human life that

I believe must be answered within the realm of the spiritual. What is the meaning of my life? Where have I come from and where am I going? What are my purposes and concerns? Where will I get guidance and strength to see me through my sorrows? What are my gifts and how do I share them? I believe we must turn to the spiritual leaders of the world for the answers.

I have a vision of recovery for humanity. I am excited by the numbers of people who are abandoning the dark and frightening archetypes of addiction in favor of recovery. My work as a therapist helps me in my own transformation. I hope it also serves to help others who want to understand the meaning of addiction in themselves and those they love. I think it is God's will for me to contribute to the world by guiding others from the darkness that addiction brings, helping them to transform addiction to new life.

Our personal myth, then, has its roots deep within our own experiences, yet just as deeply connects us in some way to the collective that has given us our uniqueness. Personal mythmaking can help us identify the values that guide our lives. We can't copy our values from someplace else; they have to come from what we know best, from what lies deep within us. We will most likely find that the values our personal myth yields are those we would most want to live our lives by.

As we come to understand the role and purpose of archetypes, mythic themes, and the sacred pattern in our lives, a deep appreciation for the commonalities we share may grow. As we become more open to other people, their experiences, and their views, we may even see that differences are only skin deep, that beneath these we really are more alike than we thought.

## NOTES

1. Campbell, *The hero with a thousand faces*, p. 25.
2. Eliade, *The myth of the eternal return*, p. 136.
3. Jung, *Psychological reflections*, p. 317.
4. Jung, *The spirit in man, art and literature*, p. 82.
5. Neihardt, *Black Elk speaks*, p. 6.
6. Jung, *Memories, dreams, reflections*, p. 5.
7. Campbell, *The masks of god*, Vol.4 p. xx.
8. Filmed interview, *Rollo May on Existential Psychology* (1976), American Personnel and Guidance Association.
9. Hatcher and Martin, *The Baha'i faith*, pp. 84–95.
10. May, *The cry for myth*, pp. 287–92, 298–302.
11. Johnson, *Femininity lost and regained*, pp. 95–97.
12. Russell, *The global brain*.

# 7

## *Giving Others Their Story: Doing a Life Story Interview*

A life is not 'how it was' but how it is interpreted and reinterpreted, told and retold.[1]

We all have a story to tell about the life we are living. As we listen to someone else's life story, we are struck by the power the story carries. This power is much like *orenda*, the magic power within traditional stories, and it makes telling a life story to another person a kind of spiritual endeavor, just as is autobiographical writing, because people get to the heart of who they are and tell what is most significant to them. They transmit their personal truth through their life story.

An experience equally powerful to writing your own autobiography or personal myth is interviewing someone else for their life story. When we assist someone else in this personally sacred endeavor, it can be not only one of the most enjoyable and rewarding interpersonal experiences possible to participate in, it can also be a way of empowering others by guiding them to a deeper understanding of their own life.

I did my first life story interview over twenty-five years ago. It was for a master's thesis in folklore, and I spent many wonderful weekends with Harry Siemsen, a Catskill Mountains farmer and singer, sitting at his kitchen table with him recording his life and his songs. I was most moved by his willingness to share his life with someone he hadn't known before and how well I felt I got to know him in the process. The deep, personal connection that was established with him, and many others I have interviewed since, has meant a great deal to me over the years.

It is impossible to anticipate what a life story interview will be like, not so much for how to do it but for the power of the experience itself. I find this to be the case over and over with my students who report how meaningful it was for them to have done the interview, especially when it was with someone they were already close to, like a parent or spouse. Just witnessing, really hearing, understanding, and accepting, without judgment, another's life story can be transforming.

A woman who had just completed a life story interview with her father wrote afterwards,

> Sitting with my father for three hours listening to his life story was a wonderful experience for both of us. Our relationship has not been one of sharing feelings and innermost thoughts. I've always felt that he loves me, although he has seldom shown his love through words or behavior. What started out to be a slightly uncomfortable experience for both of us ended up being a very special time. It was like we had both been lifted out of our worlds and placed in this room together. Of course, I would have liked to hear more about how he felt about different life events, but I know that he shared more with me that day than he had in my entire lifetime. At the end of our three hours together we hugged each other. Our eyes both filled up and then this special time ended, although the effects of this time together will stay with us both. I was allowed see my father from the inside out—and I am thankful for this.

As an approach, or method, for understanding individual lives and really connecting with another's experience, there may be no equal to the life story interview. A person telling their own story reveals more about their own inner life than any other approach could. A life story is the story a person tells of their entire life experience, remembering, or choosing to remember, as much about their life and background that they feel is important now and want others to know about them. Historical reconstruction may not be the primary concern in a life story; what is important is how people see themselves at this point in their lives, and how they want others to see them.

The life story provides a clear and ordered record of a personal truth that, of necessity, consists of both "fact" and "fiction." This is the most we can ask of a life story. No one can tell everything, or tell it all like it really was, for the eighty, fifty, or even twenty years they have lived. The life story is a personal explanation or justification for what that person has done with their life. It sets the record straight, often in a very touching way, in the person's own words.

In the description of the key experiences of a lifetime, from conflicts to transitions to accomplishments, we get much more than the mere recitation of either fact or fiction, we get personal definitions of what it means to be caught in a moral struggle, what it is like to succeed or fail, and what it feels like to witness the unfolding of one's own destiny. In the telling of their story, we get a good glimpse of how and why the various parts of a life are connected, and what gives the person their meaning in life. There may be no better way to answer the question of how a person gets from where they began to where they are now in life. A life story offers a vast array of the human qualities and characteristics that make us all so fascinating and fun to listen to.

Some people are ready at the slightest hint of another's interest to tell their life story. This may even happen in the course of everyday conversation. Others, however, may need much more prompting or even prodding. I believe that for the vast majority of people the sharing of their life story is something that they really want to do. All that most people usually need is someone to listen to them, or someone to show an interest in their story, and they will welcome the opportunity to speak autobiographically.

For those who may be reluctant, for reasons of being intimidated, embarrassed, shamed, or simply unsure about it or uncomfortable with it, here are a few of the many valuable benefits of sharing a life story:

1. We gain a clearer perspective on our own experiences and feelings, which gives greater meaning to our life.
2. Clarity about our lives gives us greater self-knowledge and a stronger self-image and self-esteem.
3. We get to share our cherished experiences and insights with others.
4. We can gain great joy, satisfaction, and inner peace in sharing our story with others.
5. Sharing our story is a way of purging, or releasing, ourselves of certain burdens and validating our own experience; it is in fact central to the recovery process.
6. Sharing our story helps connect us to the greater human community we are a part of, and may show us that we have more in common with others than we thought. In transmitting our personal truth, we also validate the collective truth we all share.
7. Our stories can help other people see their lives more clearly or differently, and perhaps be an inspiration to change something in someone else's life.
8. Those closest to us will get to know us and understand us better, in a way that they hadn't before, and probably love and respect us more for it.
9. We may even gain a better sense of how we want our story to end, how we could give it the "good" ending we want. By understanding our past and present, we also gain a clearer perspective on our goals for the future.

Doing a life story interview involves the following steps: pre-interview planning and preparation; the interview itself—guiding a person through the telling of their life story, recording it on either audio or video tape; transcribing the taped interview, with questions and comments by the interviewer and repetitions eliminated (this leaves only the words of the person telling their story so that it becomes a flowing, connected narrative); and giving the transcribed life story to the person to review and check over for any changes they might want to make. The rest of this chapter is designed to take you through these steps.[2]

What you will end up with is a flowing life story in the words of the person telling it. The only editing necessary should be to delete completely extraneous information. It may be that some shifting around of order may add to the clarity or readability of the story. If this is done, the greatest advantage to the life story interview comes into play, which is that you can consult the person whose story it is about how the story came out. They can answer the concern of whether the order or the way things seem to be connected make sense to them. The person telling their story should always have the last word in how their story ends up in written form before it gets passed around to others or published in any form.


## BASIC INTERVIEW GUIDELINES

### Decide Who You Want to Interview

The best candidates for a life story interview may be those people who emerge from our everyday interactions. They may be very close to us, we may just stumble upon them by chance, or a friend may tell us about somebody interesting. The key is zeroing in on someone who intrigues, inspires, fascinates, or perplexes you. These days, that could include people of all ages. In some cases a teenager may have just as powerful or important a story to tell as an elder. Base your choice first on whether the person touches or connects with some part of your life. If there is that kind of strong connection already between the two of you, it is likely it will be there for others, too.

Deciding on who you want to interview may be a matter of answering some or all of the following questions: Who would you like to learn more about? Who has been a model of how to live life for you? Who do you know that has overcome or learned some important things from their particular life experience? Who would you like to know better? Whose life is a mystery to you, or whose are you most fascinated by?

Maybe your grandmother is the likely choice to interview, or maybe your father. Again and again I hear from my students that the most moving life story interviews are those done with parents. There is often more shared during a life story interview between a parent and child than there has been in an entire lifetime of living together. It may even be your neighbor down the street from Afghanistan. Or it could be your niece or nephew who seems to have lived more in seventeen years than most people do in a lifetime. Who you choose to interview will always come down to who can give you some knowledge, wisdom, or insights about some aspect of life that you don't have.

### Explain Your Purpose

In advance of the interview, let the person know exactly what your purpose is. Be clear about whether it is only for you, for them and their family, or for possible publication. Let them know also that they can remain anonymous, if they wish. There are actually advantages to doing this, but if they prefer to have their name used that is their choice. Be sure they understand, too, that they will have the final say in approving any written transcript or other use of their life story.

Always respect the wishes of the person you are interviewing. Request permission to use the tape recorder (audio or video) and tell what the recording will be used for (archival, research, educational, etc.). If the tape is to be preserved in an archive, ask them to sign a release stating that they give their permission for other people to listen to the tape or read the transcript of the tape. If they would prefer to restrict the use of the material in some way, this can be worked out to your mutual satisfaction. Your compliance with their wishes, along with a supportive and encouraging attitude and your acknowledgment that you and probably others will learn some important new things from their life story, will help put them at ease and prepare them for the exciting process that lies ahead for both of you. The more sincere, assuring, and enthusiastic you are, the less convincing they will need to go along with your request.

### Take Time to Prepare

Think about what you want to accomplish. Get your thoughts, questions, and materials (tape recorder, cassettes) ready. Do as much background preparation on the person's life as possible, and, based on what you know about them, or want to know, prepare your own set of questions to take with you to the interview. Of the hundreds of questions that are suggested later in this chapter, select thirty to fifty that are most relevant for the person you are interviewing and have them ready to use when you need to ask them a question.

Be sure your equipment is operating properly. A practice session or two just getting the tape recorder working right is always wise. The tape machine is your ally; know it well and it won't become your problem. There have been many lessons learned the hard way with this one, and many good interviews that have been lost due to silly mistakes made with perfectly fine equipment. In your interview, once you have your machinery set up and going properly, you should be able to forget about it until it is time to change tapes.

The interview will be even better if you allow time for the person you are interviewing to prepare, too. They might want to freshen their memory and begin to get their thoughts organized before you come to tape their story. You could give them a sampling of six to ten questions to get them thinking about the different phases of their life.

### Use Photographs

Photographs and other objects of memory can help a person recall the stories and events of their life. If the interviewee picks out some of their favorite photographs, this will help them look back and freeze time and relive what is there in black and white (or color). Photographs may also provide further insight into the events and experiences. Those families that have preserved their children's lives in photograph albums, and today perhaps even videotapes, have a wonderful treasure to draw from when these children go about recalling and telling their life story.

### Create the Right Setting

Choose a relaxed and comfortable setting for your interview. A familiar setting, like the person's own home, is usually most appropriate. An informal room, one that is quiet and encourages sincerity, is probably the best location for the interview.

In my first life story interview, I was lucky because Harry Siemsen knew exactly where he wanted to be to tell his story. I still remember that out of all the spots in his rambling old farmhouse, he chose to do the interview right next to the wood stove in his kitchen. That was *his* spot, and it worked perfectly for the interview. Everybody probably has their own spot where they feel most comfortable, too.

Creating the setting that helps the storyteller feel comfortable is fundamental to a good interview. One approach Studs Terkel uses is to get the person involved in what is going to happen. Help them to feel needed. Even if you know your equipment perfectly, it could still help to let them help you out. The more they feel needed and a part of the process, the smoother it will go.[3] It might also help to do what you can to loosen things up for both of you before you actually begin.

Just before you do begin the interview, record your own introduction into to the tape, something like, "This is July 1, 1995, and I am interviewing Jane Clark at her home in Cornish, Maine. My name is Robert Atkinson and this is tape 95.7a." This can also serve as a final check on your equipment before you actually begin the interview. Then label side A of the tape with the same information, and you are ready to begin. Be sure you do the same thing for side B of the tape, and for tape 2, if you use two tapes.

## Get the Story

You will be assisting the person you interview to uncover and share the richness and depth that makes their life important to them. Most people enjoy having someone interested in their story. The most important thing in assuring that their story will flow easily is for you to feel comfortable with what you are about to do, and try to relax!

The amount of time it will take to get the whole story can vary greatly; anywhere from an hour and a half to eight or ten hours is a realistic rough estimate, depending on individual circumstances such as age, life experiences, personality type, and talkativeness.

## Use an Open-ended Interview

You might try encouraging the person to follow a "stream of consciousness" type of approach to telling their life story. That is, in carrying out the interview, allow them to "hold the floor" without interruption for as long as they can or want to on a given topic or period in their life. This can lead to more free association of thoughts and therefore deeper responses. For this approach, an open-ended interview in which you have specific questions ready to ask only when needed, is most appropriate. After you've explained your approach to the person, you might start out by saying something like, "Where would you like to begin the story of your life?" Then, as their flow winds down, you always have your prepared questions to draw on to lead them into another topic. If they tend to ramble on too long, and get into some areas that are not really relevant to *their* life story, you may have to pull them back on course gently and respectfully. If you use yes-no questions, you may have to follow them up with reason-why questions. Remember that in the right context, you can ask almost anything. But if you misperceive the context, the wrong question may close things down completely.

It is important to remember, as Studs Terkel points out, that preset questions can be the downfall of an interview.[4] If you come with pat questions, and follow them precisely in the interview, the answers will very likely be pat and only skim the surface. You should know when to depart from what you had planned and enter into a free-flowing conversation with the person that will capture even more of what they want to tell you.

## An Interview is Not a Conversation

An interview is like a conversation, but it is not a conversation. An interview should be informal and loose, like a conversation, but in an interview the other person is the one doing the talking. You are the one doing the listening. Your knowledge and your voice should remain in the background, primarily providing support and encouragement. An interview should have a clear beginning, as does a rite that separates ritual time from regular time. An interview also permits you to ask questions in greater detail than you would in a normal conversation. An interview has a mode of its own that allows for, on the one hand, far greater depth, and, on the other, an explanation of the obvious.

### Be Responsive and Flexible

The best technique is to be sincerely interested in what the other person has to say and to show it! Look at them, respond to what they have to say, and enthusiastically convey your interest and curiosity to them in whatever way feels most comfortable and natural to you. You can be very encouraging to the other person with nods and smiles. When they sense a mutual awareness on some topic or experience, that will help them feel a solidarity with you that can naturally lead to their telling you more than they might someone else.

There may be times when expressing astonishment or surprise at something they say could lead to an integral part of the story being explained in more detail that might have been skipped over otherwise ("How did you manage to get through that?"). When the person says something that is not clear to you, be sure to ask them for clarification ("I don't understand."). If you don't understand it, it is likely that someone else won't either.

Your role may need to switch from being a guide to being a follower when you sense a new level of excitement in what they are talking about. This is when it is important to be flexible and allow them to express what is most exciting to them about their life. It is better to let them finish what is most interesting to them than to cut this off or change the topic. It is also important to be flexible enough to pursue new and interesting topics when they come up that you hadn't thought of before. But don't forget that there may come a time for you to get them back on track.

### Be a Good Guide

You are the guide for the journey the two of you are embarking on. A good guide is on the lookout for signals about when to ask another question, when to ask more about what has already been said (or meant), and when to go on to a new topic. There may be a point when they are looking for you to ask them to elaborate on something they have just said. They may not be sure themselves if they have said enough on the topic or if you really are interested enough for them to go deeper. At times like these, you will have to use your best judgment to decide whether to ask them directly to go further. A good guide is sensitive to the times when they might have said all they want to about a topic. A good guide is reassuring. Sometimes, after they have completed a thought, it may be very helpful to let the person know that you think what they have said was clear, meaningful, or insightful, if indeed it was.

## Listen Well

To be the best listener possible is your primary objective as an interviewer. Listening to another person is neither easy nor passive. Listening is hard work that takes concentration and focused attention. Listening to another's life story means being a witness to what they are saying. It means really caring about what they have to tell you. It is possible that you may have a history with the person you are interviewing and, for whatever reason, a bias toward them in some way. Listening well means suspending that prior history, giving them your complete respect, and being as objective as possible in the interview.

Being a good listener in life storytelling is like operating a two-way radio. No matter how hard you try to make it otherwise, only one person can talk at a time. The person talking holds down the speaking button and the other person can only listen. When the person speaking is finished, you know it because they say "over and out." Then it is your turn to speak. Speaking by two-way radio uses an agreed-upon method that everyone involved understands. This method can become like a spiritual principle when it is understood, accepted, and adhered to strictly. Life storytelling could be like that. The person telling their story wouldn't say "over and out" each time they have completed a thought, but it should be clear that they are holding the speaking button down and that you are the attentive listener.

The idea of only one person speaking at a time has worked very well in the American Indian tradition of the talking stick. A sacred stick, placed in the center of the circle, is taken up by the one who has something to say and held until the speaker is finished, while everyone else listens intently, never interrupting. In this way is the speaker shown respect. When the stick is placed back in the center, another person can pick it up and speak. The person telling their story might be seen as holding the talking stick.

Using your listening skills most effectively means knowing that your storyteller has an important story to tell, that they want you to be there as an active, interested listener, and that you have something very important to learn from them by just listening to them. When you listen well, you make them feel important, which makes possible the really deep connections with them that will enable you to identify similar feelings and experiences that the two of you may share. Listening well also means having an openness to their personal wisdom, however it may have come to them.

If you listen well, a bridge of trust can be built between you and the person telling their story. Listening well produces a safe place built upon the twin pillars of trust and acceptance. There can be no room for making judgments of any kind. Listening well means caring for, respecting, and honoring the other person's life and story. Listening well is both an art to be learned and a gift to be given.

### Emotions Will Emerge

Recalling different memories will arouse all kinds of feelings and emotions. You will be of most help to the other person if you are sensitive to and accepting of whatever is going on for them, and acknowledge that. Don't worry if they pause. A silence, even a complete stop for a few moments, can be time they may need for further reflection, a time for letting inner thoughts come out. It is better to wait than to interrupt a silence. In fact, a few moments of silence can be a means of encouraging the person to speak in more detail and depth about the topic, or maybe even express feelings and emotions directly.

It would be better to ask the difficult, emotionally laden questions later, after they have gotten used to the idea of talking about their life with you, rather than in the beginning of an interview. It is never appropriate to push a person further than they are ready to go with a topic. Respect the boundaries they present, and remember to be supportive. If it feels appropriate to you, or necessary to them, after the interview is over, you can reassure them of your understanding.

### Look for Connections

Life stories offer a unique way of understanding development across time. Viewing a life as a whole is one of the important ways of highlighting the meaning of a life. Ask yourself: How can I assist this person in recognizing the overall meaning or significance of their life? How can I help this person get at what shapes and guides their life? How can I help this person express their personal truth? True sensitivity and compassion is required for you to make it seem natural for them to reach deep inside themselves for their meaning, for the clues to what has given their life significance and caused it to unfold the way it has.

### Be Grateful

When you finish each interview session, be sure to let the person know that you see what they have offered as a valuable gift. Let them know that it will be of value to others as well. And be sure to thank them.

At the end of a taping session, when you have more to complete of your interview, you might offer to have the person you interviewed hold onto the tape. There are two good reasons for this: it will help build trust between you, and it will also create a clearer sense of privacy and confidentiality between you. If you ask them to keep it in a safe place until you finish the interviews, they will know no one else will hear the tapes until they feel comfortable with it. You may want to stress that the tapes are theirs first, and they should only let others hear them, or have the tapes go into an archive, when they are ready. This could also give them a chance to review the tape, as well, if they want. If you will be returning for another interview session, you can give them a preview of what topics or aspects of their life you plan to talk about next. After the entire interview is completed, you can write a note of appreciation to them.

## Be Organized

After you have the interview recorded, you want to be able to use it effectively and efficiently. After you are finished, double checked that you have all sides of all your tapes properly labeled, numbered, and identified. As you review the tapes, make a written outline or summary of the content on each side of each tape you have used. This will make your transcription of the interview easier.

The most time-consuming part to this whole process is the transcription. If your goal is to assist the person in having their life story in a readable, flowing narrative, you can save time by skipping over your own questions and transcribe only their words. When you have transcribed the entire interview, you can then assist them even further by helping them organize the flow of their story in the way that makes the most sense. Making sure that the tapes and the transcript are preserved in a safe place is the final point to remember.

## QUESTIONS YOU CAN ASK

The questions that follow cover the entire life course and are presented in chronological order (from childhood through adulthood) within a thematic framework (covering one topic or theme in depth at a time). Using this way, those that prefer to carry out the interview by life stage (chronologically) can still do so. The thematic arrangement allows you to focus on any one area you might want to delve into more. For example, if you are interested in the person's role in local history, you can develop that theme further by focusing on what was going on in their world or community. Or, if you would like to assist someone in telling their spiritual autobiography, you can focus on the important thoughts, feelings, and meanings of their life.

These questions are given only as suggestions, and are definitely *not* meant to be fired off in rapid succession, one after the other. They are possible questions, covering many aspects of a person's life, that you can draw from. They provide a direction for you to pursue, if and when the person being interviewed has exhausted a topic. You should not feel bound by the questions at all; they are here only if you need them. Some people may require only a green light—a listening ear—to begin and carry their life story to its completion. Others may need periodic questions to keep their story going. It is often the case that the fewer questions you ask in a life story interview, the better.

You should go over all the questions here first, and familiarize yourself with them.[5] Then think of the person you have chosen to interview and decide how you want to adapt some of the questions suggested here to fit this person. Some questions may not apply at all; in other cases, you may have to add some of your own questions that you know should be asked of your person. Having a presorted list of questions to take to the interview, but being able to adapt to your situation and person, is the key here.

### Preliminary Opening Exercises

As a way of assisting the person you are interviewing to think about their life story in advance, you could ask them for a brief life summary before the interview actually takes place. This can be a helpful way to begin the process with a focus, regardless of the age or experience of the person being interviewed. Other approaches you can use to help them prepare ahead of time would include:

1. Drawing a timeline of their life that highlights and identifies the key events year by year.
2. Drawing a collage of their life on newsprint or poster paper that represents in some creative fashion the important events, experiences, and feelings in words, symbols, and images.

This type of beginning may be helpful to those people who have lived a long, full, or complex life, and who need to recall the major threads in their life before launching into a story of their life. Other people can begin at the beginning and recall everything as they go along.

### Birth and Family of Origin

One thing that makes each of us special is the particular circumstances we are born into. The genes we acquire from each parent have a lot to do with this. Who our parents are have a great deal to do with who we become. Our genetic makeup at birth has more to do with how we react to the specific world around us than we might think. It can be very important in our really knowing ourselves to know the circumstances of our family of origin. The more we know about what was going on around us at the time of our birth, the more we will know about who we have become. It might be that what we bring to the situation we are born into has more to do with determining how we adapt to things around us than do the things themselves. Here are some questions that might help us understand some of these things.

What was going on in your family, your community, and the world at the time of your birth?
Were you ever told anything unusual about your birth?
Are there any family stories told about you as a baby?
Do you remember anything about your first year of life?
What characteristics do you remember most about your grandparents?
    What do you like most and least about them?
How would you describe your parents?
    Your mother's personality, and emotional qualities?
    Your father's?
    What are some of the best and worst things about them?
    What do you think you inherited from them?
    What feelings come up when you recall your parents?
What is your earliest memory?

### Cultural Setting and Traditions

Perhaps the next strongest influence on us after genetic makeup is our cultural heritage. This will be stronger for some than others, but we all have some cultural background that is either actively or passively passed on to us as children. In some families, cultural traditions are more central to daily life than in others. This is also where our family's beliefs, values, and religious customs usually originate. We also get direct or indirect messages from our family that may have their origin in our cultural frame of reference. Culture can be the source of healthy as well as unhealthy viewpoints and patterns we adopt and carry out in our lives.

What is the ethnic or cultural background of your parents?
Were there any stories of family members or ancestors who emigrated to this country?
Was there a noticeable cultural "flavor" to the home you grew up in?
What was growing up in your house, or neighborhood, like?
    What was the feeling of this cultural setting for you?
What are some early memories of cultural influences?
What family or cultural celebrations, traditions, or rituals were important in your life?
Was your family different from other families in your neighborhood?
What cultural values were passed on to you, and by whom?
    What beliefs or ideals do you think your parents tried to teach you?
    What was your first experience with death?
    What was that like for you?
Was religion important in your family?
    How would you describe the religious atmosphere in your home?
    Did you attend religious services as a child, as a youth?

What was that like for you?
Was religion important to you as a child, as a youth?
Were there any religious ceremonies that you observed?
Is religion important to you now?
What cultural influences are still important to you today?
How much of a factor in your life do you feel your cultural background has been?

### Social Factors

As the sphere of influence upon us widens, new elements from our community, social structure, and mass culture have a greater impact on us. We begin to experience things from a wider radius that are not only new but also confusing and even in conflict with what we have been given at home. Our added experience in the social world can either stimulate, deter, or deprive us of our growth. Experience is the meaning-maker in our lives. However we face life—either directly, sideways, or with our back to it—is how we are shaped by life. Our experience of the world around us is what changes us.

Did you feel nurtured as a child?
Were you encouraged to try new things, or did you feel held back?
What do you remember most about growing up with, or without, brothers and
    sisters?
Did you get along with your family members?
Did your parents spend enough time with you?
    What did you do with them?
What were some of your struggles as a child?
What was the saddest time for you?
How was discipline handled in your family?
What would you pick out as the most significant event in your life up to age twelve?
Did you make friends easily?
    What childhood or teenage friendships were most important to you?
What pressures did you feel as a teenager, and where did they come from?
    Did you tend to go in for fads, or new styles?
Were you athletic?
What clubs, groups, or organizations did you join?
Did you enjoy being alone, or was that too boring?
What did you do for fun, or entertainment?
Was social class important in your life?
What was the most trouble you were ever in as a teenager?
What was the most significant event of your teenage years?
What was being a teenager like? The best part? The worst part?
What was your first experience of leaving home like?
What special people have you known in your life?
    Who shaped and influenced your life the most?
    Who are the heroes and heroines, guides and helpers in your life?
    Who most helped you develop your current understanding of yourself?
What social pressures have you experienced as an adult?

Were you in the military?
    What was this experience like?
How do you use your leisure time?
Is a sense of community important to you? Why? How?


## Education

Most of us get some kind of education at home, whether we are aware of it as such or not. We all get some amount of education in our community schools and beyond. For some, education can become a means to a fulfilling, and even better, life. For others, it may be just a matter of what we are supposed or have to do. However we view education, the informal as well as formal settings in which we receive an education become the matrices for many of our most important experiences in life. And for all of us, education continues throughout our entire life. This is how we continue to grow and become mature and wise. Experience, the way we understand it, and especially the way we understand our interactions with others, becomes our perpetual teacher.

What is your first memory of attending school?
    Did you enjoy school in the beginning?
What do you remember most about elementary school?
    Did you have a favorite teacher in grade school? In junior high? In high school?
    How did these teachers influence you?
What are your best memories of school?
    What are your worst memories of school?
    What accomplishments in school are you most proud of?
How far did you go with your formal education?
What do you remember most about college?
What organizations or activities were you involved with in school? In college?
What was the most important course you took in school or college?
    The most important book you read?
What did you learn about yourself during these years?
What has been your most important lesson in life, outside of the classroom?
What is your view of the role of education in a person's life?


## Love and Work

It was said by Freud that the two characteristics of a mature adult are the ability to love and to work. By mid adolescence, we may begin to get some sense that our life has some reason or purpose beyond being taken care of by our parents. We really need to explore who we are at our essence, so we know what we can do with our lives, and who or how we can love another person intimately. This begins the process of becoming independent so that, in love and in work, we can become interdependent with the others in our lives. These are also themes that we carry with us throughout the rest of our lives, though the forms and shapes may change as we do.

Do you remember your first date? Your first kiss?

Did you have a steady boy/girlfriend in high school?

When you were growing up, was it a struggle for you to match your own attitudes toward sex with those of society?

What was the most difficult thing about dating for you?

Are you married?

How would you describe your courtship?

What was it about her/him that made you fall in love?

What does intimacy mean to you?

Do you have children?

What are they like?

What role do they play in your life?

What values or lessons do you try to impart to them?

What have been the best and worst parts about marriage?

Is there anything else about your marriage you would like to add?

Did you have any dreams or ambitions as a child? As an adolescent?

Where did they come from?

What did you want to be when you were in high school?

Did you achieve what you wanted to, or did your ambitions change?

What were your hopes and dreams as you entered adulthood?

What events or experiences helped you understand and accept your adult responsibilities?

How did you end up in the type of work you do/did?

Has your work been satisfying to you, or has it been something you had to put your time into?

What is important to you in your work?

What comes the easiest in your work?

What is most difficult about your work?

When did you realize you had become an adult?

Do love and work fit together for you in your life?


## Historical Events and Periods

Each of us is born into a particular historical moment. Some moments in time may seem more significant or noteworthy than others, but each moment has its place and purpose. One of our purposes may be to understand the time in which we live, how historical events have shaped our world, our lives, and how we, all of us, shape the major events that occur during our lives. Each of us has a role on both sides of this equation that makes history what it is in our lives.

What was the most important historical event you participated in?

Do you remember what you were doing on any of the really important days in our history? (the turn of the century; the first airplane flight; the Titanic; World War I; women's voting rights; Lindbergh's flight across the Atlantic; prohibition; the stock market crash of 1929; the Depression; Pearl Harbor; the atomic bomb; the polio vaccine; the civil rights movement; President Kennedy's assassination; Viet Nam; Martin Luther King's assassination; the moon walk; Watergate; Earth Day;

nuclear protests; the fall of the Berlin Wall; the Persian Gulf war; the end of the Cold War)

What is the most important thing given to you by your family?

What is the most important thing you have given to your family?

    To your community?

Do you recall any legends, tales, or songs about people, places, or events in your community?

What is different or unique about your community?

Are you aware of any traditional ways that families built their buildings, prepared their food, or took care of sickness?

What did your work contribute to the life of your community?

What has your life contributed to the history of your community?

## Retirement

Retiring from a job or career often means a brand new phase and style of life. There is usually much more time on our hands, and we either continue doing what we were doing or find something else to take the place of what we retired from. It is a time of new ventures, more leisure, and either a greater variety of activities or a quieter routine that could become boring. In any case, these years should not be left out of a life story, as they often represent a time of increased reflection.

What was retiring from work like for you?

    Did you miss it, or were you glad to have it over?

How do you feel about your life now that you are retired?

What do you do with your time now?

Is there anything that you miss about your work?

What is the worst part about being retired?

    What is the best part?

Have all your children left home?

    How is it having an empty nest?

Do you have grandchildren?

    Do you like spending time with them?

    What do you enjoy most about your grandchildren?

    What do you enjoy the least?

    What do you hope to pass on to your grandchildren?

## Inner Life and Spiritual Awareness

An inner life, for some, is the essence of life. What goes on inside us is often more vital than what is happening around us. It can often be our reflections, our contemplations, and our inner thoughts that guide and direct what we do next, or even how our life is carried out. Many people feel that we carry within us a higher self that is guided by love, wisdom, detachment, compassion, and courage. It is important to express our understanding and experience of this part of us, as well.

How would you describe yourself as a child?
Do you think you had a happy childhood?
    What was your happiest memory from childhood?
Did you feel loved as a child?
Did you have any deep thoughts, or inner dreams, as a teenager?
What was it like to turn Thirty? To turn Forty? To turn Sixty?
Did you ever have any doubts about achieving your goal in life?
What are the stresses of being an adult?
What transitions or turning points did you experience as a teenager? As an adult?
What changes have you undergone since forty? Since fifty (or beyond)?
What role does spirituality play in your life now?
Have you ever had a "spiritual experience"?
What is most important to you about your spiritual life?
How do your spiritual values and beliefs affect how you live your life?
Have you ever felt the presence of a spiritual guide within you?
    How has this guide helped you?
Has imagination or fantasy been a part of your life?
Do you feel you have inner strength?
    Where does that come from?
In what ways do you experience yourself as strong?
    How would you renew your strength, if you felt you were really drained?
What values would you not want to compromise?
Do you feel you are in control of your life?
What single experience has given you the greatest joy?
Do you feel at peace with yourself?
    How did you achieve this?

## Major Life Themes

It is always better to end a life story interview with a few questions that help us reflect back over the whole of our lives. Taking a look at our lives as a whole will give us a better understanding of what the major themes and influences of our lives have been.

What gifts (tangible or intangible) are still important to you?
What were the crucial decisions in your life?
What has been the most important turning point in your life?
Have there been any mistakes in your life?
How have you overcome or learned from your difficulties?
How do you handle disappointment?
Are you satisfied with the life choices you have made?
What has been the happiest time in your life?
    What was the least enjoyable time?
What relationships in your life have been the most significant?
    How would you describe those relationships?
Has there been a special person that has changed your life?
What have been your greatest accomplishments?
Are you certain of anything?
What are some things you hope you never forget?

Is there anything in your experience of life that gives it unity, meaning, or purpose?
How do you feel about yourself at the age you are now?
What is your biggest worry now?
In what ways are you changing now?
What has been the greatest challenge of your life so far?
What has been the most awe-inspiring experience you ever had?
What one sentiment or emotion makes you feel most deeply alive?
What matters the most to you now?
What do you wonder about now?
What time of your life would you like to repeat?
What was the most important thing you have had to learn by yourself?
How would you describe yourself to yourself at this point in your life?
Is the way you see yourself now significantly different than it was in the past?
How would you describe your world view?

### Vision of the Future

It can be very important, and even liberating, to reflect deeply on what you really want for your own life that is yet to come. It can be a way of creating the ending to your story that you would be most comfortable with. It can also put into clearer perspective what is left to do with your life before it is too late.

When you think about the future, what makes you feel most uneasy?
What gives you the most hope?
Is your life fulfilled yet?
What would you like to achieve so that your life will seem fulfilled?
What do you see for yourself in the future? In five, fifteen twenty-five years?
What do you want most to experience before you die?
How long do you believe you will live?
How would you like to die?
What three things would you like said about your life when you die?
Do you have any advice or wisdom for the younger generation?

### Closure Questions

It is also good to make it known when you feel you are coming to the end of the interview. A question or two that lets your storyteller know you are ready to bring it to a closure and that gives them the opportunity to add some final thoughts to what they have said will facilitate the process.

Is there anything that we've left out of your life story?
Do you feel you have given a fair picture of yourself?
What are your feelings about this interview, and all that we have covered?

When you have asked all the questions that you want to, and they are satisfied that you have together covered the story of their life well, then you can bring final closure to the interview process by commenting, in your own words, how important and meaningful the experience has been for you; that you are grateful to them for all they have shared with you; that you now have a permanent record of their life story and that this will be of real value to others, as well. You could also remind them that after the tape is transcribed, they could go over the typed transcript with you for final approval, and make any changes or corrections, if necessary.

Perhaps most important, when you have actually completed the life story interview, you will know firsthand what this experience is like, that it really is one of the most powerful person-to-person interactions possible. It is an experience that both of you will treasure and one that will stay with you for a long, long time to come. And you will know that you have acted upon your own knowledge of the power of stories by giving the gift of stories to another.

## NOTES

1. Bruner, Life as narrative, p. 31.

2. Other sources for interviewing ideas are: Allen and Montell, *From memory to history*; Dunaway and Baum, *Oral History*; Fletcher, *Recording your family history*; Goldstein, *A guide for field workers in folklore*; Ives, *The tape-recorded interview*; Jackson, *Fieldwork*; and Spradley, *The ethnographic interview*.

3. Hofer, Studs Terkel: Hungry for stories, *Storytelling Magazine*, Summer 1991, pp. 12–15.

4. Ibid.

5. Other sources for interview questions include: Akeret, *Family tales, family wisdom*; Gould, *The writer in all of us*; Keen and Fox, *Your mythic journey*; McAdams, *Power, intimacy and the life story*; Moffat, *The times of our lives*; Sullivan, *The mystery of my story*; and Wakefield, *The story of your life*.

# Afterthoughts

There is a common folktale motif that illustrates how things can get very complicated when we give a gift to another.[1] As the stories go, one person sells a prized possession to buy a wonderful gift for another, only to find out that the other has changed something in order to have a gift for the other, which renders both gifts useless. But the problem always resolves itself when they realize it was their deep love for each other that they wanted to give in the first place, because this is what lasts the longest. Sometimes we spend a great deal of time trying to decide what gift to give someone, only to realize that the greatest gift is all the time within us.

Stories are the time-tested form that best convey our emotions, our deepest feelings, the values we live by, and the meaning of life, all of which are motivated by love. When there is love, the story of that love is almost impossible to keep to oneself. Story is the voice of love, and love shapes this story.

Stories are a spiritual and eternal gift. They are intangible; they can't be seen, only felt. They are timeless; they don't come and go. The message, meaning, and emotion of a good story stays with us forever. Stories convey the heart and soul of what life is about and what it can be. They are nourishment to that eternal part of us. They instruct by leading us from our own, or someone else's, past to our future. They renew by giving us hope that things can and will be different than they once were. Stories heal by letting us know that it is honorable to accept what was. Story bears a medicine that is as strong as any other.[2] In fact, the kind of medicine stories most often reflect is homeopathic, where like cures like. Some of the best stories tell us about someone else's suffering. Yet such stories can be powerful remedies for helping us bear our own sufferings.

Stories are not a panacea, however. No one thing can cure everything. It is impossible to predict how a particular story will affect someone. The same story may touch one person very deeply while for another it might not mean a thing. Expectations affect results. Overstating the potential of anything can be a setup for disappointment. There may be one occasion when a story heals and another occasion when it does not.

Even though professional storytellers don't all agree on what stories can and cannot do, the important point seems to be that storytelling *is* fulfilling some very real needs for people: the need to use the imagination, the need for community, the need for sharing personal truth.[3] Because of these human needs, people are turning—and returning—to storytelling. We seem to have a renewed appetite for real, living stories.

Story was the original form in which a community remembered and told its history. Story was the original form in which a community passed on its values and spiritual lessons. Story is an essential archetype of the human experience. And today, stories still tell us who we are while connecting us to a world much larger than ourselves. They can transform our lives if we are open to their power, if the time is right, and if the person telling or hearing the story is ready.

Giving yourself your own story is giving yourself the gift of wholeness, of spiritual health. One woman didn't want to remember her birth. Her mother was "so depressed at the event that she couldn't care for me for six or eight weeks." She went on to realize that her mother's abandonment of her had something to do with the issues of her day (the 1950s). That for her mother, having children meant giving up her true self. The woman concluded her story with this thought:

> As I grow, I can see her humanness as a reflection of my own. And in this seeing, I can forgive us both. P.S. Thank you for this exercise. It is another healing gift in my journey.

Universalizing your story is sharing the gift of what life is really like. Another woman wrote, after completing her personal myth:

> I understood the concept of universal themes and the sacredness of stories early on. However, I marveled at the truth of these notions after writing my own story and listening to the stories of the others. Originally I felt that I had next to nothing in common with this diverse group. I had not experienced the tragedies nor suffered the alienation that they wrote and spoke of. How then, would their stories be anything like mine? But they were. I was able to relate in some way to each of the stories I heard. Love, struggle, denial, loss, recovery, optimism, self reliance. . . . I could find the threads of

my story within theirs. As a result, I am viewing others and their stories much differently than I once had.

Giving others their story is sharing the heart of life with another. One woman interviewed a close friend for her life story. After the many intense hours they spent together, she wrote of the experience:

> It was invigorating and yet sobering as I was given the opportunity to look within this person's soul and spirit. The accounts of her existence captivated my interest in a fascinating way not merely because of the friendship we share but because they were genuine pieces of a life filled with meaning and vitality. Her story seemed to flow much like poetry as I listened with appreciation. As I glimpsed at the new as well as familiar aspects of her life, I could not help but compare them to my own. The geographical, cultural, and religious differences are recognized; however, the vivid similarities are far more pronounced. My life and Marsha's life are beautifully filled with real treasures. Life to us is kind. Life is plentiful and good. Life is a celebration.

Many life storytellers I have worked with have talked about how powerful and transforming are the processes of telling one's story and witnessing someone else's. Our own story is among the greatest of gifts we have to give another.

The importance of giving of oneself is central among American Indian groups. The Lakota include generosity as one of their four primary values. In the traditional "give-away" ceremony, deserving people are honored by sacrifices made by others in their name. Participation in the "give-away" is symbolic of the value placed on human relationships; they are of more importance than the material things being sacrificed. Generosity is akin to compassion for all beings.[4]

The story that comes from the heart stays with the listener the longest. When we "give- away" the stories in our heart, only then do we know how rich we really are. As our story lives on in the heart of others, love and gratitude for what we have given them grows and expands to yet others. We share the gift of our story not so much for our own purposes but for the greater purpose of the lasting bond between human beings that is created through the sharing. Our story is a gift for the ages.

## NOTES

1. See Estes, *The gift of story*, p. 25.
2. See Estes, *Women who run with the wolves*, pp. 462–64; and Estes, *The gift of story*, p. 4.
3. See Cunningham, *Do we ask too much of storytelling?* pp. 20–23.
4. See Atkinson and Locke, *Children as sacred beings*.

# References

This list includes examples of autobiographies, journals, and memoirs, theoretical perspectives on viewing life-span development in story form, and resources helpful in understanding the power of stories and the roles of sacred stories, archetypes, and mythic themes in our lives, as well as how to do life story interviews and how to write autobiographically.

Adams, Kathleen. (1990) *Journal to the self: Twenty-two paths to personal growth*. New York: Warner.

Akeret, Robert. (1991) *Family tales, family wisdom: How to gather the stories of a lifetime and share them with your family*. New York: Morrow.

Allen, Barbara, and Montell, Lynwood. (1981) *From memory to history: Using oral sources in local historical research*. Nashville, TN: American Association for State and Local History.

Allport, Gordon. (1942) *The use of personal documents in psychological science*. New York: Social Science Research Council.

Anderson, Sherry Ruth, and Hopkins, Patricia. (1991) *The feminine face of God: The unfolding of the sacred in women*. New York: Bantam.

Angelou, Maya. (1990) *I shall not be moved*. New York: Knopf.

Atkinson, Robert. (1974) *Songs of the open road: The poetry of folk-rock and the journey of the hero*. New York: New American Library.

———. (1985) *Life outcomes: Elderhood in a bicameral culture*. Ann Arbor, MI: University Microfilms International.

———. (1990) Life stories and personal mythmaking. *Journal of humanistic psychology*. Summer, pp. 199–207.

———. forthcoming *Seasons of the soul: A personal myth*.

Atkinson, Robert, and Locke, Patricia. (1995) Children as sacred beings. In *Creating racial harmony in the classroom*. Springfield, MA: Whitcomb.

Baldwin, Christina. (1990) *Life's companion: Journal writing as a spiritual quest*. New York: Bantam.

Bateson, Gregory. (1972) *Steps to an ecology of mind*. New York: Ballantine.

Bateson, Mary Catherine. (1990) *Composing a life*. New York: Plume.

Bellah, Robert, Richard Madsen, William M. Sullivan, Ann Swidler, and Steven Tipton. (1985) *Habits of the heart*. New York: Harper Perennial.

Bettelheim, Bruno. (1977) *The uses of enchantment: The meaning and importance of fairy tales*. New York: Vintage.

Birren, James. (1987) The best of all stories. *Psychology today*. May: 91–92.

Birren, James, and Hedlund, Bonnie. (1987) Contributions of autobiography to developmental psychology. In Nancy Eisenberg (ed.), *Contemporary topics in developmental psychology*. New York: John Wiley, 394–415.

Bly, Robert. (1990) *Iron John: A book about men*. Reading, MA: Addison-Wesley.

Bolen, Jean Shinoda. (1985) *Goddesses in everywoman: A new psychology of women*. New York: Harper & Row.

————. (1989) *Gods in everyman: A new psychology of men's lives and loves*. New York: Harper & Row.

Bridges, William. (1980) *Transitions: Making sense of life's changes*. Reading, MA: Addison-Wesley.

Bruner, Jerome. (1986) *Actual minds, possible worlds*. Cambridge: Harvard University Press.

————. (1987) Life as narrative. *Social research*, 54.

————. (1990) *Acts of Meaning*. Cambridge: Harvard University Press.

Butler, Robert. (1963) The life review: An interpretation of reminiscence in the aged. *Psychiatry 26: 65–67*.

Campbell, Joseph. (1949) *The hero with a thousand faces*. Princeton: Princeton University Press.

————. (1970) *The masks of God*. Vol. 4, *Creative mythology*. New York: Viking.

————. (1972) *Myths to live by*. New York: Viking.

Campbell, Joseph (with Bill Moyers). (1988) *The power of myth*. New York: Doubleday.

Cech, John (retold by). (1979) The storytelling stone. *Parabola* 4 (4): 12–14.

Chapman, Anne. (1993) Once up a time . . . *Yoga Journal* (July / August): 53.

Chinen, Allan B. (1989) *In the ever after: Fairy tales and the second half of life*. Wilmette, IL: Chiron.

Cohler, Bertram. (1982) Personal narrative and the life course. In P. B. Baltes and O. G. Brim, eds. *Life span development and behavior*. Vol. 4. New York: Academic.

Coles, Robert. (1989) *The call of stories*. Boston: Houghton Mifflin.

Csikszentmihalyi, Mihaly. (1990) *Flow: The psychology of optimal experience*. New York: Harper Row.

Csikszentmihalyi, Mihaly, and Beattie, Olga. (1979) Life themes: A theoretical and empirical exploration of their origins and effects. *Journal of humanistic psychology* 19 (1): 45–63.

Cunningham, Marge. (1993) Do we ask too much of storytelling? *Storytelling magazine*. Fall: 20–23.

Daniel, Lois. (1991) *How to write your own life story: A step by step guide for the non-professional writer*. Chicago: Chicago Review Press.

Dante Alighieri. (1949) *Divine comedy*. Baltimore: Penguin.

Diel, P. (1980) *Symbolism in Greek mythology: Human desire and its transformations*. Boston: Shambhala.

Dillard, Annie. (1989) *The writing life*. New York: Harper Collins.

Downing, Christine. (1987) *The goddess: Mythological images of the feminine*. New York: Crossroad.

———. (1991) *Mirrors of the self: Archetypal images that shape your life*. Los Angeles: Tarcher.

Dunaway, David, and Baum, Willa (eds.). (1984) *Oral history: An interdisciplinary anthology*. Nashville, TN: American Association for State and Local History.

Duncan, Isadora. (1927) *My life*. New York: Liveright.

Edwards, Carolyn M. (1991) *The storyteller's goddess*. San Francisco: Harper Collins.

Eliade, Mircea. (1954) *The myth of the eternal return, or Cosmos and history*. Princeton: Princeton University Press.

———. (1958) *Rites and symbols of initiation*. New York: Harper Colophon.

———. (1959) *The sacred and the profane*. New York: Harcourt, Brace & World.

———. (1963) *Myth and reality*. New York: Harper Colophon.

Erikson, Erik. (1950) *Childhood and society*. New York: Norton.

———. (1975) *Life history and the historical moment*. New York: Norton.

Estes, Clarissa P. (1992) *Women who run with the wolves*. New York: Ballantine.

———. (1993) *The gift of story: A wise tale about what is enough*. New York: Ballantine.

Feinstein, David, and Krippner, Stanley. (1988) *Personal mythology*. Los Angeles: Tarcher.

Field, Joanna. (1988) *A life of one's own*. Los Angeles: Tarcher.

Fletcher, William. (1983) *Recording your family history*. New York: Dodd, Mead.

Frank, Anne. (1952) *The Diary of a young girl*. New York: The Modern Library.

Franzke, Erich. (1989) *Fairy tales in psychotherapy: The creative use of old and new tales*. Toronto: Hogrefe & Huber.

Goldberg, Natalie. (1986) *Writing down the bones*. Boston: Shambhala.

Goldstein, Kenneth. (1964) *A guide for field workers in folklore*. Hatboro, PA: Folklore Associates.

Gould, June. (1989) *The writer in all of us: Improving your writing through childhood memories*. New York: E. P. Dutton.

Gould, Roger. (1978) *Transformations: Growth and change in adult life*. New York: Simon and Schuster.

Grimm, The Brothers. (1968) *Grimm's fairy tales*. Chicago: Follett Publishing Co.

Guthrie, Arlo. (1989) My oughtabiography. *Rolling Blunder Review* November: 2.

Guzie, Tad and Noreen Monroe. (1986) *About men and women: How your "great story" shapes your destiny*. New York: Paulist Press.

Hammarskjold, Dag. (1964) *Markings*. New York: Knopf.

Hatcher, William, and Martin, J. Douglas. (1989) *The Baha'i faith: The emerging global religion*. San Francisco: Harper & Row.

Heilbrun, Carolyn. (1988) *Writing a woman's life*. New York: Ballantine.

Hillesum, Etty. (1981) *An interrupted life: The diaries of Etty Hillesum 1941–43*. New York: Washington Square Press.

Hillman, James. (1979) A note on story. *Parabola* 4 (4):43–45.

Hofer, Maria. (1991) Studs Terkel: Hungry for stories. *Storytelling Magazine*, Summer, pp. 12–15

Homer. (1961) *The Odyssey*. Translated by Robert Fitzgerald. New York: Doubleday.

Hughes, Elaine. (1991) *Writing for the inner self*. New York: Harper Collins.

Ives, Edward. (1974) *The tape-recorded interview: A manual for field workers in folklore and oral history*. Nashville, TN: University of Tennessee Press.

Ives, Edward, ed. (1986) Symposium on the life story. *Folklife annual*, 154–176.

Jackson, Bruce. (1987) *Fieldwork*. Chicago: University of Illinois Press.

Jacobi, Jolande. (1959) *Complex archetype symbol in the psychology of C. G. Jung*. Princeton: Princeton University Press.

———. (1965) *The way of individuation*. New York: Meridian.

———. (1973) *The psychology of C. G. Jung*. New Haven: Yale University Press.

Jelinek, Jane Holden. (1978) *Yaqui women: Contemporary life histories*. Lincoln: University of Nebraska Press.

Johnson, Robert. (1986) *Inner work*. New York: Harper & Row.

———. (1990) *Femininity lost and regained*. New York: Harper & Row.

Josselson, Ruthellen, and Lieblich, Anna. (1993) *The narrative study of lives*. Newbury Park, CA: Sage.

Jung, Carl. (1955) *Modern man in search of a soul*. New York: Harcourt, Brace.

———. (1958) *The undiscovered self*. New York: New American Library.

———. (1961) *Memories, dreams, reflections*. New York: Vintage.

———. (1970) *Four archetypes*. Princeton: Princeton University Press.

———. (1971) *The spirit in man, art and literature*. Princeton: Princeton University Press.

———. (1973) *Psychological reflections*. Princeton: Princeton University Press.

———. (1979) *Word and image*. Edited by Aniela Jaffe. Bollingen Series No. 97. Princeton: Princeton University Press.

———. (1980) *The archetypes and the collective unconscious*. Princeton: Princeton University Press.

Kaminsky, Marc (ed.). (1984) *The uses of reminiscence: New ways of working with older adults*. New York: Haworth.

Keen, Sam. (1988) The stories we live by. *Psychology today*, December, pp. 43–47.

———. (1991) *Fire in the belly: On being a man*. New York: Bantam.

Keen, Sam, and Fox, Anne Valley. (1989) *Your mythic journey*. Los Angeles: Tarcher.

Kennedy, Rose. (1974) *Times to remember*. New York: Doubleday.

Kierkegaard, Soren. (1953) *The living thoughts of Kierkegaard*. Edited by W.H. Auden. New York: McKay.

Kotre, John, and Hall, Elizabeth. (1990) *Seasons of life*. Boston: Little, Brown.

Krippner, Stanley, and Aanstoos, Christopher (eds.). (1990) *Personal mythology: Psychological perspectives. The humanistic psychologist*. Special issue. Summer.

Langness, L.L., and Frank, Gelya. (1981) *Lives: An anthropological approach to biography*. California: Chandler & Sharp.

Larsen, Stephen. (1990) *The mythic imagination: Your quest for meaning through personal mythology*. New York: Bantam.

Levinson, Daniel, Charlotte N. Darrow, Edward B. Klein, Maria H. Levisnson, and Braton McKee. (1978) *The seasons of man's life*. New York: Ballantine.

Lindbergh, Anne Morrow. (1975) *The gift from the sea*. New York: Norton.

Maxwell, Florida Scott. (1979) *The measure of my days*. New York: Penguin.

May, Rollo. (1975) Values, myths and symbols. *American journal of psychiatry* 132 (7): 703–706.

———. (1976) *Rollo May on Existential Psychology*. (Flim) American Personal and Guidance Association.

———. (1991) *The cry for myth*. New York: Norton.

McAdams, Dan. (1985) *Power, intimacy and the life story: Personological inquiries into identity*. New York: Guilford.

———. (1993) *The stories we live by: Personal myths and the making of the self*. New York: Morrow.

McAdams, Dan, and Ochberg, Richard (eds.). (1988) Psychobiography and life narratives. *Journal of personality*. Special Issue. 56 (1) (March).

Metzger, Deena. (1992) *Writing for your life: A guide and companion to the inner worlds*. San Francisco: Harper.

Moffat, Mary Jane. (1989) *The times of our lives: A guide to writing autobiography and memoir*. Santa Barbara, CA: John Daniel.

Moore, Robert, and Gillette, Douglas. (1990) *King, warrior, magician, lover: Rediscovering the archetypes of the mature masculine*. San Francisco: Harper Collins.

Morrison, Toni. (1983) Interview with Claudia Tate. In Claudia Tate, ed., *Black women writer's at work*. New York: Continuum.

Murdock, Maureen. (1990) *The heroine's journey*. Boston: Shambhala.

Murray, Henry A. (1938) *Explorations in personality*. New York: Oxford.

Murray, Henry A. (ed.). (1960) *Myth and mythmaking*. Boston: Beacon.

Myerhoff, Barbara. (1992) *Remembered lives: The work of ritual, storytelling, and growing older*. Ann Arbor: University of Michigan Press.

Neihardt, John. (1959) *Black Elk speaks*. New York: Simon and Schuster.

Olney, James. (1972) *Metaphors of self: The meaning of autobiography*. Princeton: Princeton University Press.

Olney, James (ed.). (1980) *Autobiography: Essays theoretical and critical*. Princeton: Princeton University Press.

Pachter, Marc (ed.). (1979) *Telling lives: The biographer's art*. Philadelphia: University of Pennsylvania Press.

Pearson, Carol. (1986) *The hero within: The six archetypes we live by*. San Francisco: Harper & Row.

———. (1991) *Awakening the hero within*. San Francisco: Harper Collins.

Peseschkian, Nossrat. (1982) *The merchant and the parrot: Mideastern stories as tools in psychotherapy*. New York: Vantage.

Polster, Erving. (1987) *Every person's life is worth a novel*. New York: W. W. Norton.

Progoff, Ira. (1975) *At a journal workshop*. New York: Dialogue House Library.

Rainer, Tristine. (1989) *The new diary*. Los Angeles: Tarcher.

Rico, Gabriele. (1983) *Writing the natural way*. Los Angeles: Tarcher.

Runyan, William McKinley. (1982) *Life histories and psychobiography: Explorations in theory and method*. New York: Oxford University Press.

Russell, Bertrand. (1926) *On education*. New York: Norton.

Russell, Peter. (1983) *The global brain: Speculations on the evolutionary leap to planetary consciousness*. Los Angeles: Tarcher.

Sampson, Anthony and Sally. (1985) *The Oxford book of ages.* New York: Oxford University Press.

Santa-Maria, Maria. (1983) *Growth through meditation and journal writing: A Jungian perspective on Christian spirituality.* New York: Paulist Press.

Sarton, May. (1973) *A world of light: Portraits and celebrations.* New York: Norton.

————. (1978) *A reckoning.* New York: Norton.

Sartre, John Paul. (1956) *Being and nothingness.* New York: Philosophical Press.

Simpkinson, Anne and Charles. (1993) *Sacred stories: A celebration of the power of stories to transform and heal.* San Francisco: Harper.

Solly, Richard, and Lloyd, Roseann. (1989) *Journey notes: Writing for recovery and spiritual growth.* San Francisco: Harper & Row.

Spence, Donald. (1982) *Narrative truth and historical truth: Meaning and interpretation in psychoanalysis.* New York: W. W. Norton.

Spradley, James. (1979) *The ethnographic interview.* New York: Holt, Rinehart and Winston.

Stevens, Anthony. (1982) *Archetypes: A natural history of the self.* New York: Quill.

Stone, Elizabeth. (1988) *Black sheep and kissing cousins: How our family stories shape us.* New York: New York Times Books.

Storr, Anthony. (1988) *Solitude: A return to the self.* New York: Free Press.

Storr, Anthony (ed.). (1983) *The essential Jung.* Princeton: Princeton University Press.

Sullivan, Paula F. (1991) *The mystery of my story: Autobiographical writing for personal and spiritual development.* New York: Paulist Press.

Titon, Jeff. (1980) The life story. *Journal of American folklore* 93 (369) pp. 276–92. University Press.

Tolkien, J.R.R. (1964) *Tree and leaf.* London: George Allen & Unwin.

Turnbull, Colin. (1980) *The human cycle.* New York: Simon and Schuster.

Turner, Victor. (1969) *The ritual process: Structure and anti-structure.* Ithaca: Cornell University Press.

Ueland, Brenda. (1938) *If you want to write.* Saint Paul, MN: Graywolf.

Underhill, Evelyn. (1911) *Mysticism.* New York: Dutton.

Vaillant, George. (1977) *Adaptation of life.* Boston: Little, Brown.

van Gennep, Arnold. (1960) *The rites of passage.* Chicago: University of Chicago Press.

Vasina, Jan. (1985) *Oral tradition as history.* Madison: University of Wisconsin Press.

Von Franz, Marie-Louise. (1970) *An introduction to the psychology of fairytales.* New York: Spring.

————. (1982) *Interpretation of fairytales.* New York: Spring.

Waddington, Conrad. H. (1957) *The strategy of the genes.* London: Allen & Unwin.

Wakefield, Dan. (1990) *The story of your life: Writing a spiritual autobiography.* Boston: Beacon.

Watts, Allan. (1963) *The two hands of God: Myths of polarity.* New York: Braziller.

Welty, Eudora. (1983) *One writer's beginnings.* New York: Warner.

White, Michael, and Epston, David. (1990) *Narrative means to therapeutic ends.* New York: W. W. Norton.

White, Robert. (1975) *Lives in progress: A study of the natural growth of personality.* New York: Holt, Rinehart and Winston.

Whitfield, Charles. (1987) *Healing the child within.* Deerfield Beach, FL: Heath Communications.

Whitmont, Edward C. (1982) *The return of the goddess.* New York: Crossroad.

Witherell, Carol, and Noddings, Nel. (1991) *Stories lives tell: Narrative and dialogue in education.* New York: Teachers College Press.

Woolger, Roger and Jennifer. (1989) *The goddess within: A guide to the eternal myths that shape women's lives.* New York: Ballantine.

Zinsser, William (ed.). (1987) *Inventing the truth: The art and craft of memoir.* New York: Book of the Month Club.

———. (ed.) (1988) *On writing well.* New York: Harper and Row.

# Index

**About the Author**

ROBERT ATKINSON is Associate Professor of Human Development in the College of Education and Director of the Center for the Study of Lives at the University of Southern Maine.